Growing together

For Pippa,
who has taught me so much
over thirty-five years together

Related titles from Church House Publishing

- Growing Together: the course

- Making the most of weddings

- Pocket Prayers for Marriage
  Compiled by Andrew and Pippa Body

- Your marriage in the Church of England leaflet

Growing together

a guide for couples getting married

Andrew Body

CHURCH HOUSE
PUBLISHING

Church House Publishing
Church House
Great Smith Street
London SW1P 3AZ

ISBN 978 0 7151 42417

Published 2005 by
Church House Publishing.
Second edition 2007
Fourth impression 2016
Copyright © Andrew Body 2005, 2007
Illustrations © Paul Airy 2005

Cover design by ie Design Consultancy
Printed and bound by CPI Group (UK) Ltd, Croydon, CR0 4YY

Contents

Acknowledgements

Extracts from *The Works: Selected Poems* by Pam Ayres reproduced with the permission of BBC Worldwide Limited. Copyright © Pam Ayres 1992.

Extract from the *Collected Poems of T. S. Eliot* reproduced with the permission of Faber and Faber.

Extract from *Too Many Songs* by Tom Lehrer reproduced with the permission of Methuen Publishing Ltd.

Extracts from *Common Worship: Pastoral Services* reproduced with the permission of the Archbishops' Council.

Extract from *Poems* by Steve Turner copyright © 2002 Steve Turner. Used by permission of Lion Hudson plc.

How to use this book

Don't read it from cover to cover

The King's advice to Alice in Lewis Carroll's *Alice in Wonderland* is the usual way to read books:

> *Begin at the beginning, and go on till you come to the end; then stop.*

However, this book is different. It would be good to begin at the beginning, with the introductory chapter 'Affection, lust and love', and it would be good to end with the final chapter, called 'Ingredients of the wedding cake', which is different because it is a practical guide to ways in which you can plan your wedding service. But what you do in the middle is entirely up to you. The chapters are arranged alphabetically, and not in any order of importance. You can read them in any order you prefer.

Read it one chapter at a time

This book takes a dozen topics and approaches them in three ways:

- what attitudes and prejudices we may have inherited from our upbringing and past;

- what our present experience has to tell us;

- what hopes and fears we have as we look into the future.

Questions are provided to get you thinking and talking. Some of them will be irrelevant to you – others may occupy you for a long time.

Read it separately and then together

Like some dishes in restaurants, this is 'for two people'. To get the most out of it, each of you needs to read a chapter, and then share the things it has raised for you. Compare notes on your individual answers to the questions and see how much you think the same way. Even deciding in which order to take the chapters could provoke some interesting discussions! If you have talked long and hard about the particular subject, you can feel good that you have done so. If another part of what is written here opens up ideas you have not had the opportunity to share, then that must be a good thing as well.

Read it slowly

The purpose of the book is to help you think – so give yourselves plenty of time. Read the text of the chapter before tackling the questions and don't miss out questions just because they are difficult! They might just be the most important for you to think about.

Use it as part of your formal marriage preparation

Ideally, if you are getting married in church, you will be offered some kind of marriage preparation. It may be that you have been given this book by whoever is undertaking that with you, whether as an individual couple or as part of a group of couples undertaking the *Growing Together* course now available. In that case, you may have the chance to share some of the issues that the book has raised with someone else, and you can discuss how best that can be done. But it is most unlikely that you will have twelve sessions to share it all in detail. Much of what you talk about as a result of reading this will remain between just the two of you.

If your marriage preparation follows some other pattern, then what you get from this book will provide useful material to add to the discussion, whether it is just as a couple with the minister or other person, or whether you are part of a group.

Come back to the book from time to time

You will be sharing your hopes and fears for the future. Maybe not every year, but from time to time, as your anniversary approaches, revisit particularly the questions about 'Where are you going?' – and see how far you have got on your journey together.

Affection, lust and love – an introductory chapter

We shall not cease from exploration
And the end of all our exploring
Will be to arrive where we started
And know the place for the first time.

(T. S. Eliot, 'Little Gidding')[1]

You are reading this, presumably, because you are in love and are thinking about getting married. I have been asking couples for over 30 years what they mean when they say that they are 'in love' and, with my hand on my heart, I can say that I have never had the same answer twice. That is because we are trying to put into words a set of the most intense feelings that any of us ever experience. Even with the help of poets and song-writers, we find that hard to do. We use the word to refer to our favourite drink, to our favourite colour as well as to the deepest relationships we ever have – with our parents, our children, with God, and of course with our life-partner. With such a complicated idea, it is not surprising that the Bible uses at least three different words to express it – translated roughly in the three words in the title of this chapter. They are all important and positive ingredients of what 'love' means.

Some people enjoy analysing things, and others find that deadening. Putting your love under the microscope may sound a dreadful thing to do, and I am not suggesting you do that. But what I am certain about is that, if you explore what you mean by being in love, you have the potential to enrich it even more. As people come to their wedding day, they can't imagine that they could ever love each other more than they do at that moment. But the reality is that, if their love is what they say it is, it will go on growing and they will be even more in love as the years go by. This book is an invitation to exploration of the unique journey on which you have embarked.

Marriage is an exciting and adventurous enterprise that is different for everyone. 'No one in their right mind can tell anyone else how to be married.' I have often said those words to couples getting married and I stand by them. So what is this book about? This is not a compendium of the right answers to all the issues that might arise – it is a guide to asking some of the right questions.

'Marriage is an exciting and adventurous enterprise that is different for everyone.'

People getting married today are asking many more questions than their parents and grandparents did. Surrounded by people whose relationships have not lasted, they are anxious not to join their number. Usually approaching marriage from a time of living together, they are much more closely in touch with the things that can make and mar permanent relationships.

Happily, more and more couples are being offered opportunities to reflect on what they are doing. The old expression 'marriage preparation' is beginning to be replaced by 'marriage exploration'. That is an improvement, because it rightly implies that marriage is an ongoing process of becoming, rather than a state we enter suddenly one Saturday afternoon. A young man once said to me 'I shall never stop getting married.' Asked to explain, he pointed to words in the wedding service that say 'All that I am I give to you'. 'But I don't know all that I am yet', he said, 'and when I discover more, I'll have to marry that bit as well.' That was a wonderful insight and something that applies to people of any age. We never stop getting married – or rather, we *shouldn't* ever stop getting married.

So maybe these chapters and questions will also be useful to people who have been married for some time, to help them reflect on their love for each other. But their main purpose is to help those about to 'commit matrimony', whether they are living together already or not. Although marriage is 'a gift of God in creation', as the Church of England's marriage service says, each generation has to work out what it means in its time and culture. Comparing the way marriage was for people even 50 years ago shows how true that is.

This book is written by someone who does believe marriage is God's gift. All faith communities have things to offer in understanding marriage but none of them 'owns' marriage.

And, although this book is written by a Christian, it is for people with little or no faith as well as those who are committed believers. It is not trying to push a particular line or doctrine but, amongst other things, offers some perspectives of faith for you to make of what you will. Jesus never cornered people, but he did challenge them. I hope you will find that this book does something of that for you.

The people mentioned in this book all exist. Their identities have been thoroughly disguised, but the vicar mentioned is me. They are some of the hundreds of couples with whom I have had the privilege to share the months before their wedding. I want to thank them for all they have taught me, and hope that their stories may now teach something to others. I also want to thank Sue Burridge from the Archbishops' Council, and especially a group from the Mothers' Union in the Guildford Diocese (Corinne Cooper, Ann Fraser, Prue Young and Canon Dr Michael Hereward-Rothwell) for their support, encouragement and help.

Something to talk about and share

■ **What do you mean by 'being in love'?**

Children

[Marriage] is given as the foundation of family life in which children are born and nurtured.

(Preface to The Marriage Service, p. 105)

By the time they get to their wedding day, most couples will have honestly discussed their feelings about wanting to have a family. But, amazingly, some have not. Rather more only discuss it superficially and, finding that they have differing views, avoid the subject, often on the basis that the other one will change his or her mind eventually.

Recent medical advances have the potential to give couples choice in planning their families. But each advance means a further set of choices. Contraception comes in various guises and every couple has to make the choice of what suits them best. If there are problems in conceiving, there is plenty of help to be had – but, again, it raises complex choices about what is right for each couple. The increasing number and accuracy of prenatal tests may raise enormous questions about what to do if some serious abnormality were predicted. For all good things there is a price to be paid, and couples today need far more skills to help them make appropriate choices than their parents ever did.

Babies are born into all sorts of family situations. There is no doubt that cohabiting couples and single parents are often superb at their job of nurturing their offspring. But there is now growing scientific evidence that, in various ways, children who come from stable marriages do better than their contemporaries. One of the functions of marriage seems to be to provide the most appropriate nest-building in which the next generation can thrive.

At the end of the day, those who do want to have a family, and are able to do so, would find themselves in sympathy – most of the time – with the writer of the Psalm who said, two and a half thousand years ago:

> *Children are a heritage from the Lord*
> *And the fruit of the womb is his gift.*
>
> *(Psalm 127, The Marriage Service, p. 149)*

In their less pious moments, and particularly as children get older, they may have sympathy for Ogden Nash:

> *Children aren't happy with nothing to ignore*
> *And that's what parents were created for.*
>
> *(from 'The Parents')*

Where are you coming from?

Every one of us is both the beneficiary and the victim of our parents. They not only gave us life, but they also gave us our initial way of seeing life. The process of growing up includes making proper judgements about what was good and bad in our upbringing. Hopefully, most of us don't end up feeling as negative as the former Poet Laureate Philip Larkin. In his celebrated poem 'This be the verse', he expressed in no uncertain terms that however well-intentioned our parents are, they mess up our lives. They hand on to us some of the faults and prejudices they inherited from their parents and then add more of their own for good measure. This is an extreme view, but his words are a reminder in strong language of how much our parents influence us. You can easily find the whole poem on the Web.

*'By the time they get to their wedding day,
most couples will have honestly discussed
their feelings about wanting to have a family.
But amazingly some haven't.'*

Craig and Jane both come from happy homes. He was the fourth in a family of five, and she was an only child. Their feelings about childhood and what it means to be a family are radically different, but both have happy memories. In their heart of hearts they both want to reproduce those good memories for any children they might have. But that is not possible: they cannot have one child and several. The decision may be made for them because of practical factors like money, but they really need to tease out what it was that made for their happiness, and how they can come to a joint decision about what they want for their own family.

Helen and Mark, on the other hand, have had very different experiences. Whilst he was part of a relaxed and supportive family, she grew up in a succession of foster homes, some of which were loving and healing for her, but the last of which

7

was a place where she was abused by another child. She could not bear the thought of being less than a perfect parent, and did not think she could live up to the standards she would set herself. So she was dubious about having children at all. He was much more laid back, and knew from his experience that children can cope well with the rough and the smooth, and longed for the family life he knew himself.

The combinations of backgrounds are endless. Every couple has its unique mix. But, unless you really talk about what your childhood has meant, you are less able to make good decisions about what you want for yourselves. You may not be in touch with both your parents. You may not know who one or both of them is. You can idealize both about what you had and what you never had.

Things to talk about and share

- **What are the best and worst memories of your childhood?**

- **What were the good and bad things about being an only child, or in having brothers and sisters?**

- **What are the things you want to be the same for your children?**

- **What things would you like to be different for them?**

Where are you now?

Let us assume for the moment that you don't have any children. At this point in your relationship, you don't want any. It takes two to have children, and ideally it takes two *not* to have them. Do you review your decisions about contraception from time to time? You probably need medical advice as well as discussing your personal preferences. Good decisions are ones made together, and not to please your partner. Sometimes when people are getting married after living together for some time, one partner assumes that this is also a signal that it is time to start a family. But that isn't necessarily so, and this would be a good time to talk again about your medium- and long-term plans.

The decision to have or not to have children will have wider implications. What will be financially possible? What will it mean in terms of employment? Will one of you give up work to be a full-time carer for your family and, if so, which one of you will it be? A few couples manage to reduce hours for both of them and job-share looking after their family. For many it will be a question of someone else taking care of the child – relatives, a childminder or a work-place nursery. Whatever the decisions, there will be huge changes to the demands on your finances, and to the freedom you have to do as you please. It is probably the most radical change in your lifestyle that you ever have, and for many couples it is stressful as well as rewarding.

Things to talk about and share

- **Do you want to have children**
  - **soon?**
  - **sometime?**
  - **never?**

- **Why have you made that decision, and does your partner share it?**

- **Are you both happy with your choice of contraception?**

- **If you have children, what are your plans for their day-to-day care?**

- **How will you cope with the increased demands on your time and energy?**

Where are you going?

We are very privileged to have the ability to plan our families. The decision about having children is often central to the dreams we have about the long-term shape of our relationships. John and Hilary want to have their children while they are young. Lucy and Michael want to develop their careers before taking time out to have a family. Hugh and Petra are so involved in their careers that they cannot see a time when having children would be appropriate for them. Louis and Freda already have five children between them and feel that having more together would make life over-complicated for everyone.

But plans don't always work out. People who don't want children find one is on the way. Most people these days have friends who are having difficulty in conceiving. The figures are quite alarming. One couple in six goes to their doctor to say they are worried. For many of them it is impatience rather than a problem but, nonetheless, the number of people who do have problems of infertility has risen sharply. There is a great deal to be said for talking *now* about how you would feel if this became your situation. If you don't discuss it until it is a hot issue, you will then be full of highly charged emotions. Talking about it now in a detached way may help you if the issue arises later. You don't have to agree later with what you said, but at least it gives you a starting point. Some couples simply want to accept the situation. Others want to look at other options like adoption or fostering. Yet others will want to pursue medical interventions of various kinds. Each of them has a price to pay – in the case of IVF treatments it may be a financial as well as an emotional price. If there is a problem, either in having or not having children, you need to be open enough with each other that you are not secretly taking or giving blame.

In some parts of the world genetic counselling is routinely offered to couples getting married. Unless there is some obvious reason, that is not so for most of us. But tests during pregnancy may reveal possibilities, of varying degrees of certainty, about potential health problems for your child. Again, it is a good idea to have talked about this kind of thing before it is for real. For some, terminating the pregnancy would be utterly unthinkable in any situation, for others it might be a possibility they would seriously consider. Between you there may be differing views. Do you know how each other thinks? It takes a great deal of trust and honesty to be able to face all this but, with increasing numbers of tests available, more and more people will be in this situation. Jill and Tony's marriage came under great strain when they discovered that he had agreed to a termination only because he thought that is what she wanted, and she had gone ahead only because she thought it was his wish.

Things to talk about and share

- **How would you feel if you had difficulty in conceiving?**

  - **What would you do in that situation?**

- **How would you feel if you found you were expecting an unplanned child?**

  - **What would you do in that situation?**

- **How would you feel if you were told you might have a handicapped child?**

  - **What would you do in that situation?**

- **How will you share the nurture and care of any children you may have?**

  - **Will you look for support from parenting courses?**

For everyone who has children, there needs to be thought about who does what. There is much evidence that, unless we consciously make decisions, we will tend to do what happened to us in our own childhood. The words attributed to King George V provide a grotesque example: 'My father was frightened of his mother. I was frightened of my father, and I'm damned well going to make sure that my children are frightened of me.' Most parents find themselves, in the heat of the moment, saying things to their children that they swore they would never say, because they hated it when it was said to them. Under strain, we tend to go back and replay the tapes that were recorded when we were small. There is a huge amount to be gained from learning parenting skills together, so that we share and support each other in a task that is the most daunting and also the most rewarding in the world. One of the prayers in the *Common Worship* marriage service puts all this on a very high plane. It says to God 'you enable us to share in your work of creation' (Prayer 23, p. 167). There is an old Jewish saying that there are three involved in the conception of a child – a man, a woman and the Holy Spirit of God. And, in nurturing our children, every home is a place for spiritual as well as physical, intellectual and emotional growth.

Commitment

. . . to have and to hold
from this day forward;
for better, for worse,
for richer, for poorer,
in sickness and in health,
to love and to cherish,
till death us do part.

(The Vows, The Marriage Service, p. 108)

Martina Navratilova, the tennis player, once said 'Do you know the difference between involvement and commitment? Think of ham and eggs. The chicken is involved. The pig is committed.' That's a good image to run with. There are plenty of relationships that are 'egg', and don't develop into 'ham'. Real commitment means no barriers, no holds barred, no reservations. It's a strange thing in the wedding service that the example offered to a couple is not a great pair of lovers of the past, but the example of a bachelor – Jesus Christ. But his love for his friends was utterly without reservation. He could easily have said, when it became apparent what might happen to him 'I love you, but . . .' But his love went as far as it could possibly go. Inappropriate as it might be for a Jew, his love was 'ham' not 'egg'.

Some people living together outside marriage have that ideal kind of total commitment. But, for many, it is conditional commitment, a provisional arrangement, providing everything continues to be good for both of them. At least, that seems to be the evidence of the many couples who say that they see marriage as a further stage of their relationship, when they will be totally committed to a lifelong partnership.

There may be something about our time in history that makes such an absolute commitment hard. Young people don't join organizations like Scouts and Guides as they used to but, on the other hand, are often eager to commit to 'causes' like environmental groups. Organizations often say that they can get volunteers who are prepared to be on standby, but find it harder to get people to promise to help regularly as a matter of priority. People opt in and out of all sorts of things. In relationship terms, that may lead to 'playing the field'. People book for evening classes, and then drop out. Airlines have to overbook in order to ensure their planes are full, because they know some people who have booked will not turn up. To say words that mean total, unambiguous commitment is against the trend. Independence is a goal many are struggling to achieve and enjoy, and that can make it hard to commit to someone else.

'Most people don't have a conscious "shopping list" when they are looking for a partner.'

But what comes from commitment is a sense of well-being and security. 'My beloved is mine, and I am his' as it says in the wonderfully erotic Song of Solomon – a book in the Bible. In days past in the UK, the belonging was horribly unequal. The wife belonged to the husband, but not vice versa. Now, as a beginning to the marriage service says, 'In marriage husband and wife belong to one another.' Each is the most precious thing the other has. To know we come first, second and last in someone else's life is the most affirming thing that can happen to us. To love and be loved makes people blossom, like a flower opening.

Where are you coming from?

A television documentary traced the stories of some children who were bought the most amazing presents, and had extraordinary amounts of money spent on them. They were not particularly happy children. One of them, faced with a parent saying that she went out to work just so she could buy all these things, said that she would prefer just to have her mum's time and attention. We all want to be needed, not tolerated. We all want to be valued, not bought. Most parents do give themselves in huge measure to their children. But often children don't realize all that their parents give up for them until they are parents themselves.

It would be good to think through all the things that made you feel secure as a child, the things that made you feel loved, the things that made you feel that you belonged. By the same token, think of the things that made you feel less secure, and what effect that had on you.

People who come from homes where there has been little sense of commitment may find it harder to feel such security in adult life – but will almost certainly crave it deeply. Ron was such a young man. He had learned he could never rely on people. His parents were more concerned for their own interests than for anything they might do as a family. His father was a workaholic, and his mother busy with a whirl of social activities. He was left with a succession of babysitters. As he grew older, he realized they were simply paid to look after him, and had no interest in him as a person. In fact, he began to wonder if he was worth knowing. He didn't seem to matter very much to anyone.

Paula and Graham had lived together for over seven years before they decided to get married. The vicar asked why they wanted marriage after such a long time. Their reply was both warming and sad at the same time. 'It's taken us all this time to feel we could risk it. We have each seen both our parents divorced twice – six divorces in all. Marriage always seemed to spell gloom and disaster. It's only after being really happy for as long as this that we can dare put the label round our necks.'

In adult life we learn the hard way that we cannot trust everyone. In different ways, people sometimes let us down. They promise something but don't keep the promise. We think we can rely on them, but find

Things to talk about and share

- **What were the things the people who brought you up committed to?**

  - **You?**

  - **Work?**

  - **Money?**

  - **Pleasure?**

- **How did that show in practical ways?**

- **How much were you expected to 'see things through'?**

- **Did people around you in your childhood keep their promises?**

- **What makes you feel secure, or insecure?**

- **Have those things any connection with things that have happened to you?**

that we were wrong. The more we are let down, the harder it is to trust someone else. That will be especially true of broken relationships that meant a lot to us. We bring those hurts into new relationships we make, in the hope of finding healing and new hope.

Where are you now?

Something remarkable has happened in your life. You probably wouldn't be reading this book unless you were on the verge of getting married. So someone has so deeply affected you that you feel able to say – 'Yes, this is the person I want to be with for the rest of my life.' No doubt you could analyse some of the reasons why they fit your bill – but most people don't have a conscious 'shopping list' when they are looking for a partner. In fact, most people are not consciously looking for a partner at all when they fall in love. It might be worth telling each other some of the reasons that you have confidence that this is the right thing to do. If you can't think of any, then maybe you have some serious thinking to do. One couple called off their wedding after they were asked why they had chosen each other. The message came – 'I couldn't think of any good reason last night to marry him, and I still can't, so we're calling it off.' People are generally not very good at telling people the positive things about why they value each other. In the old marriage service, when the ring was given, the man said 'with my body I thee worship'. Worship really means 'worth-ship'. That is why saying that you love each other matters so much. Taking stock of the things you value about each other simply adds to that. It is telling the other what he or she is worth to you.

Trust is part and parcel of commitment. It is easily lost, and only regained with great difficulty. So how much you trust each other is central. Brian and Joanna were talking about their financial arrangements. They didn't have a joint account because 'we could never trust each other enough' – not a very good omen for their marriage. If you can't trust someone with your money, can you trust them with your future? If people cannot trust each other, they are likely to be very possessive and suspicious. If people feel that is what is happening, they start to get anxious, and maybe even deceitful, in order not to feel trapped. Those are slippery slopes to be on. Jill's husband was intensely jealous, partly because he didn't think very highly of himself, knew that she was very pretty, and assumed that she would easily be enticed away by someone 'better'. She felt she had no freedom, because he demanded to know where she was all the time, and so began to find ways of escaping to have time with her female friends. Nothing she was doing could have been a cause of worry for him, but he was driving her away from him by the way he was treating her.

If you are already living together, think about what differences getting married may make. If you cannot imagine that it will make any difference to your excellent relationship, then why are you doing it? It seems an expensive way of achieving nothing. If, on the other hand, you think it will make a

Things to talk about and share

- **What do you value about each other?**
- **How do your strengths and weaknesses complement each other?**
- **Would you ever want to 'check up' on each other? Why?**
- **Is it OK to have any secrets?**
- **What difference will getting married make to you?**

difference, what will that difference be? Why does that matter to you, and what does it say about the way your relationship has already developed?

Where are you going?

The vows at the beginning of this chapter have their feet firmly on the ground. They talk about better and worse, richer and poorer, sickness and health. If you are a very unusual couple, you might stand there on your wedding day and say 'It's all going to be worse, poorer and sick.' But it is far more likely that you will be thinking it is all going to be better, richer and healthier! But the words say both. There is nothing dewy-eyed and romantic about them – they are tough words about real commitment.

Ted and Liz were a wonderful young couple. He was a fine sportsman. She was a bubbly personality who made everyone smile. But, six months into their wedding, she was

Things to talk about and share

- Have you had any health issues to face together yet?

- Can you imagine caring for your partner if they became dependent on you in some way?

- One of the prayers in the *Common Worship* marriage service says 'May they reach old age in the company of friends'.[1] How does that make you feel?

- Have you made a will? Will you be doing so when you get married?

- What inscription would you like on your gravestone?

taken seriously ill with a disease that amongst other things confined her to a wheelchair. Nothing in their marriage was like the dreams on their wedding day. Ted nursed her and cared for her for fifteen years. The week she died, he said 'I couldn't have had a happier marriage.' From the outside, anyone would have said that was nonsense. But he meant it. They were totally committed to each other, and they still had each other. That was enough for them.

Most people will have some ill health to cope with. Most people will have some poorer times, particularly if they have a family. There may be other things, like redundancies or family problems, that are the shadow side of those vows. But those words say that this is not a 'fair weather' relationship – it is an unconditional, come-what-may commitment to each other.

People spend fortunes trying to maintain their youth. There is nothing wrong in staying fit and healthy – far from it. But when the motivation is fear that, if I put on weight, or lose my hair, or in some other way become less superficially attractive, then my other half will lose interest in me, then that is a sign that commitment and trust are issues we need to face up to. The Beatles' song 'Will you still need me . . . when I am 64?' poses a real question.

The commitment is for life – 'till death us do part'. We hope that is a long time off. Share the confidence of William and Maureen, who, marrying when they were in their seventies and fifties respectively, promised a case of champagne to anyone who produced the invitation and the order of service at their silver wedding. But death is part of the reality of life. Talking about it, so that, for example, you know each other's wishes about burial or cremation, is healthy, not morbid. Making a will is a sensible and loving thing to do. If you have talked about your feelings about death, you are also ensuring that you are the best possible help to each other when either of you is bereaved as the years go by. People look to their partner more than to anyone else to be there for them at times like that, and can be dreadfully let down if their needs are not met.

> *Old age begins*
> *And middle age ends*
> *The day your descendants*
> *Outnumber your friends.*
>
> *(Ogden Nash, 'Crossing the border')*

Communication

. . . that each may be to the other
a strength in need, a counsellor in perplexity,
a comfort in sorrow and a companion in joy.

(Additional Prayers, The Marriage Service, p.158)

People communicate by speaking and listening, looking and touching, so there are at least those four skills to work at.

In the early days, there is so much to say. You don't know very much about each other, and you want to know everything. So people talk for hour after hour. How much they take in or remember may be another thing, but there is much to say! Similarly, they spend a lot of time looking at each other – mainly at close quarters. The traditional 'gazing into each other's eyes' is not just poetic licence, it is what people actually do. Every smile matters. And people touch – they hold hands, they put arms round each other, they sit close together. It is amazing how many messages you can give quite accurately just by the way you hold hands – try it and see!

But sometimes the talking is quite superficial. They may have a lot of facts to share, but maybe less communication about feelings. To say it tends to be a problem for men more than women is perhaps a very sweeping statement, but has more than a grain of truth. But both may find it hard to talk about their inner feelings. It takes patience and encouragement to risk difficult topics where you know there are sensitivities to be respected.

When things go wrong in a relationship, people often put it down to bad communications. Yet, when most people fall in love, they never stop communicating. What goes wrong? Do they have nothing left to communicate, or do they lose the art? Keeping good communication alive is well worth the effort. Pam Ayres' poem 'The husband's lament' ends:

> *We've been together twenty years today*
> *And there's a moral*
> *Since we have no conversation,*
> *We have never had a quarrel.*
> *We hardly see each other,*
> *So we never have a fight,*
> *For 'Silence it is Golden'*
> *And we've certainly proved that right.*[1]

The other half of talking is listening – one without the other is a bit pointless. Proper listening takes concentration and is a

'Keeping good communication alive
is well worth the effort.'

skill that can always be improved. Many people say that their partner doesn't understand them – and really mean that they don't feel listened to. The Children's Society a few years back ran a splendid poster campaign with the slogan 'This child needs a good listening to'. What goes for children goes equally well for adults.

Even after months or years of talking, you have only shared a bit – it would take a lifetime to share all that has happened to you both before you met – and then there is all that is happening to you now to be taken care of as well. If you are bored by each other after a short while, what is that saying about how much you really care?

And, strangely, silence of the right kind is another important tool of communication. When people are not very close, silence can be awkward, and one or other feels it necessary to break it. It is the mark of people who are good at communicating that they can also be comfortably silent together, without the need to entertain, or impress or persuade.

Ogden Nash has a splendid poem about a couple where the wife says only unimportant things when facing her husband, but tends to say anything important when she is walking away.

> *Yes, her words when weighty with joy or dread*
> *Seem to emerge from the back of her head.*
> *Knowing her custom, knowing the wont of her*
> *I spend my life circling to get in front of her.*
> ('How can Echo answer what Echo cannot hear?')

Because simple touch has developed into making love, some couples lose the art of holding hands, and other, less intimate, touching. Sex therapists working with people who have problems in their sexual relationship will often ban intercourse for a while, so that people can rediscover these other kinds of touching.

The way we speak, listen, look and touch are the raw materials of good communication. The best communicators use them all.

Where are you coming from?

Patterns of communication are often set at home. The percentage of homes where people sit round a table to eat together is surprisingly small – certainly it is the minority. People who have grown up in homes where family meals are rare may have had few role models of adult communication. If you have never experienced how husbands and wives talk to each other, how can you copy it? If the television or the radio is constantly on, there may be little chance to learn how to listen with full attention. Conversations may happen, but with the participants looking at a screen, rather than each other.

Terry and Paula had this problem. They loved each other dearly, but neither of them was very good at talking. She came from a large family where there never seemed to be time to sit down one-to-one and talk at any depth. He came from a family where neither mum nor dad could talk about feelings. When he was upset or ecstatically happy, no one seemed to want to know. The miracle was that they both realized how much they had missed out, and they set about working at how to talk to each other. They made a decision only to put the television on when they really wanted to watch a programme, and the rest of the time in the evenings, they just sat together on the sofa, and talked. For him, particularly, it was very hard to put feelings into words.

Things to talk about and share

- **What was communication like when you were young?**

- **Did you eat together?**

- **How much did you discuss what was going on?**

- **Were you encouraged to share your feelings?**

- **Do you come from a 'touchy-feely' family, or one that was very reserved?**

But the effort was rewarded with a closeness that neither of them had known before. 'We can say anything to each other,' they said. To some people that might be something taken for granted. For others, like Terry and Paula, it was a wonderful discovery.

Modern communication systems have much to commend them, but it is unlikely that people will want to keep a record of text messages saying 'lv u lts'! – whereas, in past generations, love letters were treasured and kept for a lifetime.

Where are you now?

Chris has a very demanding job that involves dealing with people all day long. When he gets home, he is anxious for some peace and quiet. His wife Jennie, who is caring for their three small children, and doesn't get much opportunity for adult conversation apart from brief encounters at the school gate, is bursting to share what has been going on and to get some stimulating conversation from him. For a time, they didn't handle those conflicting needs very well. Eventually, they were able to talk it out and negotiate a way of dealing with it that gave them both elements of what they needed. Their solution was for a few minutes of noisy madness with all the family when Chris arrived, and then he would have a shower to unwind and relax. They kept their 'adult' conversation for when the children had gone to bed, but made sure there was always time for it. They also had an evening each week when they went to the pub for a meal on their own.

Everyone's situation is unique. Chris and Jennie's will be different from yours. They will have to go on adapting their solution as children get older and other demands put new pressures on them, so it isn't something fixed and final. The vital thing was to be able to communicate their needs, and to see how far those needs could be met.

Things to talk about and share

- **What are the best and worst times for you to talk to each other?**

- **Can you agree to disagree sometimes?**

- **Are you a good listener? – and does your partner think you are?**

- **Do you think your partner is a good listener, and do they think they are?**

- **Can you always read the unspoken messages from each other that come from body language and facial expressions?**

Andy and Pat were both keen on sports. He played football, and she played hockey for local teams. Organizing babysitting for their toddler was made easier by the fact that her mum lived quite near. They were very happy that they could both enjoy their sports separately. But there were constant problems because neither of them was very good at telling the other about changes of training schedules and matches. So, time after time, they found they hadn't got their baby-sitter, and that mum was already committed to something else. The communications hadn't so much broken down, as had never been in place. They found that a kitchen wall diary was the answer for them. They each had to take responsibility for their part of things, and couldn't blame the other for not listening by saying 'But I told you . . .'

Communication has to happen at many levels, from the banal and everyday 'Do you want another piece of toast?', right through to the serious and daunting 'I've found a lump, and I am afraid to go to the doctor'. Some conversations get put off because we are afraid of how the other may react, or that we will say something we don't really mean. Choosing the right time and the right setting can sometimes be difficult. But putting it off means communications are breaking down.

Where are you going?

In a lifetime together, people ought to be getting better and better at communicating. When that doesn't happen, it is because something is getting in the way. It might not be deliberate – it could even be simple laziness. Making time for each other is an obvious basic step – if you have no time together, then it is unlikely that you can say much to each other. Weekends away may give you opportunities to talk to each other at levels you have forgotten, or never had. There are weekend courses providing a comfortable setting to think about these things, which are helpful to some.

There are many skills that can be learned and improved. Courses that people attend for other reasons – at work or for pleasure – can be brought to bear on your communications in the marriage. People find that, in doing parenting courses to help them communicate with their children, they are also improving the way they talk to their partner. For example, learning to use 'I' messages ('I feel sad when you . . .'), rather than accusatory 'you' messages can help a lot. Lessons from assertiveness training can help you say what you need and want without becoming aggressive. An evening class in massage or reflexology might enhance the range of ways in which you can communicate by touch.

Anniversaries can be a happy time to reflect on how things are changing and developing for you as a couple.

Things to talk about and share

Write your own!

His | Hers

Companionship

May the hospitality of their home
bring refreshment and joy to all around them;
may their love overflow to neighbours in need
and embrace those in distress.

(from the Prayers, The Marriage Service, p. 112)

In one of the wonderful monologues about nursery children by the late actress and comedienne Joyce Grenfell, the boy and girl playing Mary and Joseph in the Nativity Play start to fight. The teacher breaks them up with the words 'But Mary and Joseph were *friends*!' Most people's relationships start out as being simply friendship, and develop into love. That is not how it has always been. The old marriage service put companionship last in the three reasons for marriage – in those days there was no guarantee you even knew your partner, let alone were friends with them!

Yet, out of those three reasons – children, sex and companionship – it is the last that is likely to be the most significant in the later years of life. Sex will, one hopes, still be part and parcel of the relationship, but is likely to be less important in your eighties than in your twenties. If there have been children, they will have grown up and gone. But the companionship – maybe even leaning on each other literally by that stage – will remain a central pillar.

Some couples lose sight of their friendship in the fever of becoming lovers, and the exhaustion of being parents. Maintaining friendship is not only good at the time, but is storing up good things for the future as well.

Friendship is a valuable commodity. We may have lots of acquaintances, but probably not many deep friendships. In Ecclesiasticus, a book of wise sayings in the biblical Apocrypha, it says:

> *Faithful friends are a sturdy shelter; whoever finds one has found a treasure. Faithful friends are beyond price; no amount can balance their worth.*
>
> *(Ecclesiasticus 6.14-15, NRSV)*

When a couple can say of each other that they are best friends, they are paying each other an enormous compliment.

'Some couples lose sight of their friendship in the fever of becoming lovers, and the exhaustion of being parents. Maintaining friendship is not only good at the time, but is storing up good things for the future as well.'

Where are you coming from?

Everyone learns from those who bring them up, without realizing. So, in an ideal world, everyone has seen how the friendship of those people works. You will have seen how they liked to do things together, as well as apart. You will have seen them share memories, jokes, problems – all the little things that make up the ordinary bits of life. But it isn't an ideal world for others, and those patterns of companionship may not be part of what you have lived and breathed.

There will have been other friendships. Childhood friendships, and certainly friendships made in adolescence and early adult life, may be among the strongest we ever make. King James II used to call for his old shoes because they were easiest for his feet. The historian John Selden said that is why old friends are best. People who have known you well over many years can seem very close even after long times apart. They are often the people who can be most honest with us and about us.

Trust is a vital part of friendship. When someone lets you down, it hurts, but when it is a friend, that is doubly hurtful. It makes a

Things to talk about and share

- **What did you see of your parents' friendship (or of those who brought you up)?**

  - **What was the everyday glue that bound them together?**

  - **What were the things they shared?**

- **Do you have close friends from your schooldays, or from college?**

  - **What makes them special?**

- **What was special about the friendship with the person you then fell in love with?**

mockery of all that friendship stands for. So, if people have had lots of bad experiences like that, it makes it much harder for them to make friends and be a friend to others.

Where are you now?

One of the fine balancing acts for every couple is to decide how they divide time together and time apart. If there is little or no time together, that is not going to be satisfying. But people also find that being together all the time isn't a good thing either. People who work together, and spend all their leisure time together may not have much to tell each other. It lies behind those words from Kahlil Gibran, which are often read at weddings:

> *And stand together, yet not too near together:*
> *For the pillars of the temple stand apart,*
> *And the oak tree and the cypress grow not in*
> *each other's shadow.*
>
> *(from 'On marriage')*[1]

The psychologist Robin Skynner wrote a book about marriage with the title *One Flesh, Separate Persons.*[2] We do no service to each other if we cease to be the interesting people we are in the cause of becoming one rather dull common denominator. It is great to do things together, but important to do our own thing as well. Companionship means taking an interest in what each other does, but not necessarily feeling that you have to be there with them all the time.

Bob and Miranda spent virtually all their time together outside work. He rather painfully took up her hobby of riding, and she was to be found on the touchline of every rugby game he played in winter, and at the boundary of the cricket field in summer. But the price they paid was that they lost touch with many of the friends that they had before. He never went down to the pub, even after matches, and her evenings out with the girls from work stopped abruptly. It wasn't that they had forbidden each other to do these things – they just wanted to do everything together. Do you think they were doing the right thing?

Friendships give another layer of companionship that even the best marriages cannot provide. Enjoying them benefits the marriage, because we need different types of friendship to fulfil all that we might be. Is it an unreasonable expectation that your partner can be everything you need? 'Why can't a woman be a chum?' sings Professor Higgins in *My Fair Lady*. Was he right?

Things to talk about and share

- **What things do you do together?**

- **What things do you do on your own?**

  - **Have you got the balance right for both of you?**

- **Do you make time for your 'mates' as well as your mate?**

- **Do you get on with each other's friends?**

Where are you going?

Circumstances change how couples spend time together. Children's activities may make big inroads into their available energy. Increasingly, creaking joints may mean retiring from active sports. There may be opportunities to take up new pursuits together, and create new circles of friends they have in common. Companionship will take a different form in every stage of life. But whatever couples do together, they are going on growing in their friendships with each other and with those around them.

People don't live in isolation. They have neighbours and colleagues at work. There are people they meet socially. The marriage service says marriage 'enriches society and strengthens community'. A happy home has an effect not just on those who live there, but on those who are in touch with it in any way. Bob and Carole were a very happily married couple with a large family. But their home was always open to others in the village where they lived. When

Things to talk about and share

- **Are there new things you would like to do together when time allows?**

- **Can you think of ways in which you can contribute to community life where you live?**

- **What things will you continue to do, together or separately?**

people had joys to share, or needed a shoulder to cry on, their kitchen seemed to be the natural place to go. Without them, that village would have been much poorer. Every marriage has the potential for making life better for others.

Communities are only as good as the people who live in them make them, and in most places most of what is done is from the efforts of just a few people. Contributing to the community can run the gamut from giving countless hours to help run the Scouts or a playgroup, to very simple and undemanding things. Martin and Olwyn used to go to the pub most Friday evenings. Then they discovered that a home for people with cerebral palsy was desperate for people to take one of their residents out to the pub. He didn't need entertaining – but he did need transport. It was only a two minute job to collect him, but it made a huge difference to that young man's life. Those who look for volunteers find that the hardest thing is getting people to commit themselves to help on a regular basis. If one or both of you can spare an hour, weekly or fortnightly, there are bound to be people who could use your time and your skills. If you do it together, it is part of your companionship. If you are happy to do it separately, it is a way in which you share each other with the community around you, and everyone benefits. In his eighties, Alec was still treasurer of over thirty organizations in his town. He carried on because no one else seemed willing to take over. The old proverb 'Many hands make light work' is absolutely true.

Conflict

May they be gentle and patient,
ready to trust each other,
and, when they fail,
willing to recognize and acknowledge
their fault
and to give and receive forgiveness.

(Additional Prayers, The Marriage Service, p. 157)

No two people can agree about everything. You can argue that, unless there is difference, there isn't much of interest. Art depends on difference in colour, in light and shade. Music depends on the difference of sound and silence, concord and discord. Many couples thrive on the fact that they each have strengths and weaknesses – 2 plus 2 adds up to more than 4, it seems! Marriage depends in its very essence on the difference between male and female. Ogden Nash, the American humorist, said:

So I hope husbands and wives will continue
to debate and combat over everything
debatable and combatable.
Because I believe a little incompatibility
is the spice of life, particularly
if he has income and she is pattable.

(from 'I do I will I have')

What is at issue for any relationship is not so much whether you have differences, but how you differ, and how you resolve your differences – or don't! When Jesus was talking to his friends in the Sermon on the Mount, he encouraged them to deal with conflicts in a positive way, and warns that leaving things unresolved can lead to even greater problems. The whole sweep of the biblical story is about God going on and on forgiving, despite the dreadful things his people did. The more we are aware of being forgiven, both by God and by other people, the more likely it is we can be forgiving ourselves.

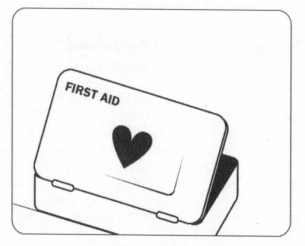

*'Think about the first aid you
have for your relationship.'*

Where are you coming from?

Chris and Helen find it hard when they disagree. What seems nothing much to Chris feels like the end of the world to Helen. He can't understand why she is so upset, and she can't see why he is so aggressive.

The roots of their problem may lie in their different experiences as children. Think about the families in which you were brought up. You may also have feelings about the ways your parents handled tensions, particularly if their marriage ended in separation or divorce. Many people feel they have been damaged by being brought up in families where there have been non-stop rows. It may make them very sensitive to any disagreements – is it a sign that you are heading in the same direction as they did? The more you have shared your feelings about all this with your partner, the less likely it is that you will get things out of focus between you. But people who have grown up in families where there has apparently been no conflict at all may be equally distorted by their experience. If you have never seen arguments being resolved in your parents' marriages, you have no role models of how it is done, and so again you may be oversensitive to the squabbles you have. Every family has its comfortable level of noise in arguments. What is normal to one family seems like a screaming match to another.

Things to talk about and share

- **What has been your experience of conflict both as a child and since?**

  - **How were tensions between the people you grew up with resolved?**

  - **How have disagreements between you and others been resolved?**

  - **What made it possible to pick up the pieces and move forward?**

  - **What prevented that happening?**

  - **Are there things which are still unresolved, and how do you feel about them?**

- **What are the things in your life stories that help and hinder resolving differences?**

  - **What is your experience of being forgiven, or not being forgiven?**

  - **How good are you at forgiving?**

Each of you also has your personal history of how conflict has been handled in your own life. Maybe you have been married before. How did that relationship end, and how has that experience coloured the way you think and feel now about disagreements and arguments? It doesn't need to have been a marriage for those things to be part of the background to how you handle conflict. Most people come to marriage after some broken relationships. Every one of them will have been a cause of how you feel about this now.

Where are you now?

Most conflicts are so slight that it almost sounds too strong to call them that – they are minor disagreements. So, most of them will be resolved unconsciously. But inevitably there will be more serious issues somewhere along the line, and it is useful to think in advance how you might tackle them. Conflicts left unresolved tend to be like balls of string in the kitchen drawer – you can't find the end and, when you pull them, it sometimes makes things worse.

It is worth comparing the repairs we might need in a relationship to the way we handle repairs to our bodies. Most people have a first aid kit in their home, or at least a collection of bits and pieces in the bathroom cabinet. If you don't, it is a good thing to put on your wedding gift list! You hope you won't need it very often, but it is good to know it is there, and what is in it. Then, when you cut your hand, you know where the plasters are.

Think about the first aid you have for your relationship. How do you get over the little disagreements? It might be in giving each other space, or time to cool down. It might be in seeing the funny side of whatever it is. It might be your ability to listen. Almost certainly you have a whole boxful of 'first aid' skills that you may not have consciously been aware of.

Sharing those skills with each other gives you the same kind of confidence that having the first aid box gives you.

But suppose the medical problem is something a first aid box won't solve. You know your next source of help is the doctor. What are the next sources of help for your marriage? Can you use your family – parents, brothers and sisters? Do you have friends whom you can trust, and who will not be put in the embarrassing position of being expected to take sides? It is good to know whom you have got, and it will be different for everyone. It will also be different depending on the issue in hand. Some things may not be appropriate to share with some of that circle of support around you.

And then suppose the medical problem is a crisis – you haven't nicked your finger, you have nearly cut it off. Then you need the local A&E Department – and fast. In relationship terms, where is that? Maybe it is your minister, maybe a counsellor, or some other professional help that is needed. Do you know where to get it? As with the A&E, it is good to know where it is in advance, so you don't waste time and effort.

There are some frightening statistics about violence in marriage. It happens to a large number of all sorts of people, and it is said that, on average, women suffer 33 incidents of violence before they seek help. Men can find it very hard to tell others when they are victims of violence. A police officer I knew was once asked if the enquiry he was on was his first 'serious murder'. His reply was 'Yes – all the others have been entirely frivolous!' All violence is potentially serious, and needs treating seriously right away.

No one can solve your problems and resolve your conflicts for you. But someone may enable *you* to do so when your first aid seems inadequate. Clergy and counsellors find that, generally, people don't seek professional help as quickly as they might. They see it as 'the last chance saloon'. That is a pity, because a single unresolved issue is much easier to tackle than a dozen. Facing up to conflict, and learning to handle it positively, is one of the most important skills we can acquire.

A surprisingly high percentage of couples comes to planning their wedding day with quite important unresolved issues. Some are just ignoring them, in the hope that they will go away (which is unlikely), or with the dream that getting married will in itself provide the magic answer (which it will not). Others find that making marriage plans makes them face up to things realistically. That is quite scary, because there is always the risk that it turns out to be so big an issue that the wedding needs to be postponed or even cancelled. Either of those can be, at the end of the day, a positive thing. If you are preparing to decorate a room, and find a huge damp patch on the wall, it is stupid to slosh the paint on regardless. Within a very short time it will look terrible again. If you do the work that is needed, it may mean the room isn't ready for when Great-Aunt Gertrude comes to stay, but it will mean that, once properly done, it will last for a good time, and she will enjoy it on visits for years

Things to talk about and share

- Are there any topics you are avoiding talking about because they might be difficult?

- What are the skills you have as a couple that are your 'first aid' when things are not perfect?

- To whom can you turn for help when you need someone to share your problems?

- Who provides a good model for you of relationships being healed?

- Have you got boundaries that must not be crossed?

to come. Even backing down completely, and calling a wedding off, is positive if your relationship has the seeds of its own destruction already growing strongly. You need to be free to move on. It is significant that the church service asks you on your wedding day whether there is any reason why you should not get married. What an extraordinary thing that is to say to a couple as they stand ready to make their vows! That question is about the legal reasons, but really it applies to anything that is a serious unresolved conflict. If there are cracks there, they will not go away by magic.

Where are you going?

Living 'happily ever after' is the stuff of fairy tales. And stuff and nonsense it is! If you envisage your life together as a line on a graph – how would it look? If you dream of a line going steadily up and up, with ever increasing bliss, then pack in your job, and write trashy novels. That is not how life is. If you think of it as a line keeping absolutely level, because you just want to be as happy as you are now, then prepare eventually to get bored with it. If the line in your imagination is plummeting down, maybe you need to think through your marriage plans again! What we can reasonably hope for is a line that does go up and up, but with some dips and hollows in it. There will be fewer good times, for even the most devoted couples. Comments about '60 years and never a cross word' are to be taken with a large pinch of salt. They may well not *remember* the cross words, because they have had so many good times. But no one gets through 60 years totally unscathed! You know how this works, when you think of people talking about their holidays. They come back saying what a wonderful time they have had. But then, later in the day, they tell you that they had a five-hour wait at the airport, and there were several days of torrential rain. What was bad was cancelled out by what was good. That is the realistic dream we should have. If we do not stay realistic, then we will tend to give up as soon as difficulties arise.

Think of your relationship as a cup and saucer. Crockery from the supermarket, if it gets cracked, will be thrown away. But if it is fine bone china, you would get it repaired. It is too precious to throw away because of a little crack. What sort of cup is *your* relationship? That picture takes us back to advice in another of Ogden Nash's verses, which says:

> *To keep your marriage brimming*
> *With love in the loving cup,*
> *Whenever you're wrong, admit it;*
> *Whenever you're right, shut up.*
>
> *(from 'A word to husbands')*

Things to talk about and share

- **How will you judge whether you have a good marriage?**

- **What will you do if you decide you haven't?**

- **How do you feel about seeking professional help if things are really wrong?**

Dreams and expectations

Give them patience with their failures
and persistence with their hopes . . .
In gentleness let them be tender with each
*   other's dreams*
and healing of each other's wounds.

(Additional Prayers, The Marriage Service, pp. 156–7)

Dreams are a normal part of living – the good ones are the things we hope will become reality, the bad ones are the nightmares we hope will not. They are sometimes quite fun, as Ogden Nash relates:

Here is a dream.
It is my dream,
My own dream,
I dreamt it.
I dreamt that my hair was kempt,
And then I dreamt that my true love unkempt it.

(from 'My Dream')

Our dreams of marriage may be quite complex. They may be quite unattainable, and fantastic. They might be quite reasonable and realistic. They might be nightmares that make us lose sleep. But, as Hammerstein's song in *South Pacific* puts it:

If you don't have a dream, how you gonna
have a dream come true?[1]

Where are you coming from?

Dreams are sometimes a way of escaping the harsh realities we face day by day. So some people bring to their marriage dreams that are about creating a good version of what has been bad in their experience. They have seen at first hand a marriage that has not been happy. But they know it doesn't have to be like that. They build up huge expectations of how their marriage will be an ideal fusion of kindred spirits, with never a cross word, and everything unfolding in ever-increasing bliss. They might make a lot of money from writing cheap novels – but they won't be able to base it on experience. They will be able to make some of the dreams come true, but not all of them. They will have to live with disappointments as well as successes.

People sometimes have expectations that are unrealistic. Advertising leads them to want a 'dream home', with every conceivable luxury. The pictures always show acres of space

'Differing expectations'

in the kitchen and wonderful flowers in the garden. The reality for most couples at the beginning of their time together is living in a cramped flat, or maybe even in a bedsit. There isn't a garden at all, and you cannot afford even some of the necessities, let alone the luxuries. Strangely enough, that is not all bad news. If all your dreams come true right away, what have you got left to dream about? Having something to aim for and work together for can give a sense of purpose and excitement that more than compensates for any making do in the here and now.

Part of the secret is working at knowing the difference between needs and wants. Jeanette admitted, as the wedding day grew closer, that she had been

Things to talk about and share

- **What were your childhood dreams of what marriage would be like?**

  - **Where did those ideas come from? (Experience? Books? Films?)**

  - **How do you handle disappointments, and not being able to have what you want, when you want it?**

  - **Are you good at deciding whether something is a 'need' or a 'want'?**

conned by all the magazine articles into thinking she needed all sorts of extras for the wedding day. They wasted a lot of money they couldn't afford. Those things were fine as long as they were seen as things that she wanted, but maybe could not have. But they had crossed the line temporarily into being 'must-haves' – and by the time she realized, the contracts had been signed. What applies to wedding days applies to everyday life as well.

Where are you now?

If you have been together for any time, you will have been working on the differences between the dreams and the realities. The dreams that are coming true will be sustaining you and encouraging you. But some of the dreams will not have come true at all, or only in part. Graham and Elaine envisaged sharing all their time together when they were not at work. But it soon became apparent that they each wanted time to be with their own friends, and to pursue their own hobbies. They found they also wanted time just to be alone. It is another example of when you have to decide whether things are 'needs' or 'wants'. Getting the right balance of time together and time apart is not always easy and, for anyone who has a jealous streak in them, the people at the sports club or the pub can seem like rivals. Maybe you envisaged making all the decisions together, but the reality is that one or other of you had to decide which lampshades to get because visitors were arriving tomorrow, and there was no time to go out together to choose them.

Some dreams have been fulfilled. Others maybe are shattered. Many will still be 'on hold', waiting for their time. Remember the poet W. B. Yeats' warning:

> *I have spread my dreams under your feet;*
> *Tread softly, because you tread on my dreams.*
> (from 'He wishes for the cloths of heaven')[2]

Things to talk about and share

- **What dreams are already coming true for you?**

- **Are there dreams that you now think will never come true? Why?**

- **In what ways is your relationship better and worse than you had imagined?**

- **Is your partner all that you hoped he or she would be?**

- **Does he or she 'tread softly' on your dreams?**

Where are you going?

If people marry at about 30, which is the average age these days, they could reasonably expect to have at least 40 years together, and probably 50. Yet it is almost impossible to imagine that length of time – even longer than you have already lived. The marriage declaration 'for as long as we both shall live' and the vow 'till death us do part' are enormous blank cheques that we sign to each other. But that is the essential nature of marriage. It does not say 'for as long as we both shall love' or 'till us do part'. So, however long you have already been a couple, there will be still more to come than you have experienced already.

The *Common Worship* marriage service talks of people 'growing together in love and peace'. Marriage is not a static thing – not just a legal status. It is a dynamic, living and changing thing that has infinite potential to make people more than their dreams ever allowed. So, as you look into the future, you go on dreaming, and working at making the dreams come true, picking up the pieces of the broken dreams that have had to be discarded, and replacing them with new ones.

Things to talk about and share

- **What are your dreams of how things will be**
  - in five years' time?
  - in ten years' time?
  - in twenty-five years' time?
- **What have you done with your shattered dreams?**
- **Do you have any nightmares that make the future look less bright?**
  - Can you do anything about them?

Faith

Marriage is a gift of God in creation,
through which husband and wife
may know the grace of God.

(Preface to The Marriage Service, p. 105)

Back in the 1920s and 30s, people used to talk about 'getting spliced'. The picture of joining two ropes together is a good one for marriage, but seems old-fashioned now. Getting a good splice means making sure all the strands are properly connected. The traditional Christian view of human beings is that we are one unit – body, mind and soul. It is pretty clear that of those three, the splicing of souls – marriage at a spiritual level – tends to be the weakest link.

You might have been tempted to skip this chapter, on the basis that you do not think of yourself as very religious. But everyone is somewhere on the line between believing nothing and believing everything. What you *don't* believe is just as important a part of the marriage as what you *do* believe. Understanding each other's faith, or lack of it, is an important part of knowing each other. It forms part of the way we see the world, and how we make all sorts of decisions.

When you started going out with your other half, you probably asked lots of questions about their friends and family. You wanted to know if they liked golf, or heavy metal, or whether they preferred Indian or Chinese food. They were happy to share the answers with you. But suppose someone were to ask (and it is most unlikely they would) what your partner's religious views are. Would you be able to answer as

'If we do have strong beliefs, we may still prefer to keep quiet about them in case anyone laughs at us . . .'

confidently as about their taste in music or food? If the answer is no, then it would be a clue that this bit of the 'splicing' is not as good as it might be. The reason is almost certainly that you haven't talked about it. That is not surprising, because most of us are not very practised at talking about our beliefs. We tend to keep them to ourselves and, if we *do* have strong beliefs, we may still prefer to keep quiet about them in case anyone laughs at us, or, still worse, tries to change them.

When the marriage service says that 'marriage is a gift of God in creation', it is going beyond the boundaries of Christianity and saying that, whatever people's religion, they are in touch with something that is part of God's purpose for all humankind. What is more, it says that marriage has the potential for being a place where we can discover things about God. It doesn't happen automatically, but it might. We can see the world with or without religious meaning. Steve Turner's 'Poem for Easter' begins:

> *Tell me:*
> *What came first*
> *Easter or the egg?*
> *Crucifixion*
>   *or daffodils?*
> *Three days in a tomb*
>   *or four days*
> *in Paris?*
>   *(returning*
> *Bank Holiday Monday).*[1]

That is why the Church has always said that marriage has a sacramental character – it is a means of encountering God in a special way. Many people who are not outwardly very religious choose to have a service to mark their marriage, rather than a civil ceremony. It is not just that it is traditional – it is their sense that this is so important, it needs a different setting from law and bureaucracy. Robin was a young man who felt that very strongly. He wasn't a churchgoer – in fact he wasn't sure what he believed, if anything. But he was clear that what he was doing in marrying Marie was something beyond what secular words could achieve. However vague his belief, he needed something that was beyond the everyday. He and Marie (who had no clear beliefs either) had to decide how their wedding plans could include that sense of 'otherness'.

Where are you coming from?

What is your religious 'heritage'? That may be a question that goes beyond what your parents believed – it may well involve grandparents and others as well. There are many young adults today who were baptized, dedicated, ritually circumcised, or whatever initiation was appropriate, not because it was important to their parents, but because their parents' parents expected it. So you may come from a religious tradition without its meaning very much in practical terms. But it might have gone deeper than that. Even if those who brought you up didn't go to church, they may have sent you to Sunday school. At the other extreme, you may come from a devout and committed religious family – Christian, Jewish, Muslim or whatever. In that case you will have accepted and rejected various aspects of those traditions and come to wherever you presently stand on matters of faith.

You will also have had some exposure to religion at school. That might have been main-stream and thoughtful – or it

---

Things to talk about and share

- **Do you believe in God?**
- **Did your family have any connections with a church**
  - **regularly?**
  - **at Christmas and Easter?**
  - **at weddings and funerals?**
  - **never?**
- **Do you pray**
  - **regularly?**
  - **occasionally?**
  - **only in church?**
  - **never?**
- **Are your beliefs different from those of the family you grew up in?**
  - **What made them change?**

may have been wildly eccentric, as in the school whose atheist headmaster dutifully had a daily assembly, but skilfully rewrote all the hymns, avoiding any mention of God! You may have felt that you had enough religion at school to last a lifetime, or you may have found a living and real faith of your own.

What goes for belief also goes for religious practice. Were you taught to pray at home? There are millions of people who pray regularly who never darken a church door. They may not even think of what they do as 'prayer' because they have got the mistaken idea that you have to kneel down and put your hands together for 'real' prayers. But when there is a crisis, or when they are over the moon about something, they find themselves talking to someone, who might or might not be God! Patrick and Joanna gave their vicar a shock when he asked them if they ever prayed. He knew neither of them had ever been churchgoers, but it turned out that, whilst Pat was away from home because of his work, they phoned each other every night and always said a prayer together. And prayer can be a secret. Mike and Rita had shared a bed for seven years before they discovered that both of them prayed every night.

Where are you now?

One of the things that you are bound to have discussed is whether you are going to have a church wedding. That is a major faith decision. It may well be that one of you has gone along with what the other wants. But it is important to maintain your integrity. Starting a marriage by saying things you don't really mean and doing things you don't want to do is not a good way to begin. Unfortunately, there is a crunch here that cannot be avoided. There is no halfway house. You cannot have a church service without religion, and the law does not permit anything religious in a civil ceremony. So you have to decide on which side of the fence you are coming down. It gets particularly complicated if you are from different faith traditions, or even from different traditions within Christianity. It is good to know that you are not the first to have to work out solutions in these circumstances, and there may be some help available from people who have wrestled with these questions before. The person who is taking your service should know people you can contact.

Sean and Alice had this problem in a big way, although the root of the problem was their family, not themselves. He came from a devout Roman Catholic family: she was Church of England. He was happy to get married in her church, and her vicar was happy to invite his priest along to take part. But that didn't satisfy his parents, who put such pressure on him to change the arrangements (despite their parish priest telling them to back off) that eventually Sean had a breakdown, and the marriage nearly had to be called off because of his ill health.

It can take courage to go with your innermost convictions. Darren and Shirley originally wanted to get married over their motorbikes in church, but the vicar pleaded that oil stains would ruin the carpet. Darren was a member of a Hell's Angels

Things to talk about and share

- How did you decide about where to get married?

- Has either of you had to give way on some aspect of what you want?

- If you had to persuade the vicar that a church wedding was appropriate for you, how would you go about it?

- Has the process of arranging a wedding changed your religious views in any way?

chapter. But, despite that, they both felt that church was the only place for a wedding. They had no hymns, because they said their friends wouldn't know any, and the congregation was exceptionally quiet, because instead of the usual ushers to show people to their places, they had a 'minder' who had a pickaxe handle up his sleeve! They married wearing their leathers, but Shirley had a little white veil attached to her helmet. To avoid possible troubles with rivals, they left church with police motorcycle outriders. It must have taken guts to go through with that. Their faith was unorthodox, but mattered to them.

Where are you going?

Faith is often talked about as a journey. On journeys we see different things as we turn each corner. So it is unlikely that any couple will go through the whole of their married life without one or both of them changing what they believe. It can happen in both directions. Paul and Fiona were very vague in their beliefs and never went to church. But, about ten years into their marriage, he had a profound religious experience that led him to be very open and active in his local church. Fiona found that very hard to cope with. She felt almost as if, in Jesus, she had a rival for Paul's affections. By contrast, Stewart and Karen had both grown up as Christians and were both very involved in their local church. When Karen had a series of miscarriages, it shocked her considerably and she began to have real doubts about God's love, and wanted to withdraw from church. Stewart felt helpless and let down that she was no longer sharing his way of seeing things.

If you have a family, some of the faith questions will become more obvious. Will your children be baptized and, if you come from different churches, in which church will the baptism take place? If you have different faith backgrounds, will you share both with your children, or choose one? Many people who don't pray on their own still think it is important to pray with their children. Is that something you will want to do?

Churches often provide the opportunity for couples to renew vows, or to meet around St Valentine's Day to give thanks for their love for each other. Some provide marriage enrichment courses and home groups where people can share their experience of marriage and family life. If you are involving God on your wedding day, it is good to ask yourself how you will involve him afterwards.

Faith and marriage have so much in common that the Bible uses the image of marriage to talk about the love of Jesus for his people – he is the bridegroom and the Church is the bride. The prophet Hosea uses the imagery of an unfaithful wife to talk about how the people of Israel were being unfaithful to God in his day and age. Growing in love for God is one way in which we may grow in love for one another. If we believe God is love, then any love, including that of husband and wife, is related to his love for us all. Faith is the way we say 'Yes' to God's proposal to us.

Things to talk about and share

- Will you ever go to church after your wedding day?

- If you have any, will your children be baptized?

Families

Weddings are among the great family occasions. Yet, while often living far from their family roots, and in very fragmented families, often with the complexities of second marriages to cope with as well, people are increasingly interested in genealogy, and spend long hours researching their family tree. The need to belong to the tribe is very deep-seated, even in our sophisticated global society.

Relations crawl out of the woodwork for weddings who are never seen or heard of at any other time. Changing times, however, mean that parents may be less involved in the planning and payment of weddings than they used to be. Couples often very properly arrange their own marriages, and invite their parents, rather than the old tradition of parents inviting the guests. On the day itself, the two family groups may have very little to do with each other – sitting on opposite sides of the church, and at separate tables at the reception.

For couples getting married, there is a sense of becoming part of another whole family. Even if you don't see a lot of each other, it feels important to most people to be accepted by their partner's family. For some it will be a chance to add to their experience of what families can mean. Greg had never known his father, so having Jo's father to relate to began to give him some echo of a relationship he had never had before, and they became very close. It was probably significant that Greg became the son that Jo's father had never had. For Kevin, becoming part of Maggie's large and close family was quite daunting. He was an only child, and had no aunts and uncles, and so no cousins either. He had no idea how to cope with all these different relationships. Maggie sometimes found it hard to understand why it was so difficult for him.

Whilst you marry each other, not each other's families, nonetheless, they come as part of the package, and how you relate to them is part of becoming a new unit within that larger group.

Where are you coming from?

What has been your experience of the wider family? Just looking at its size can give some indication of how different our backgrounds are. Gordon's family amounted to a dad (his mother having died when he was a baby), an unmarried aunt and one surviving grandparent. That's a total of four. Paula, on the other hand, had three sisters and a brother, two birth parents, a step-parent, and her father's new partner, five aunts and uncles, with their respective partners, a gaggle of twelve assorted cousins and four grandparents. That's a total of thirty-five. If you have a mathematical bent, you can work out the number of relationships there are in a family. If R stands for the number of relationships within a family, and y stands for the number of people in the family, this is how it works out:

R = y multiplied by (y minus 1) divided by 2

So, for Gordon it was 6 possible relationships (4 x 3 ÷ 2). For Paula it was 595 possible relationships (35 x 34 ÷ 2). The family we come from really does make a difference to what we might know about relating to others who are connected to us!

It is not only the differences in sheer numbers that affect our feelings about what family means. We will also have very different experiences of how close and important those relationships are felt to be. Often it is one person, or one household within a wider family, that holds them all together, keeping them in touch with what is going on elsewhere. When such a person dies, it can be catastrophic for the people who have relied on them to make family 'work'. Some people find families oppressive because their close-knit web

Things to talk about and share

- **How important has the wider family been in your life up to now?**

- **Would you describe it as 'close' or not?**

- **How many Christmas cards do you send to family members?**

- **Are there any family heroes or embarrassments?**

demands too much. Others long for a sense of belonging, and regret they have no one in the family who is interested in their doings.

Families all have their private history, and their secrets. The musical *Salad Days* has a song about the uncles of the hero. It includes the line 'There are five of them – four, and the one we don't mention'![1] We may be very proud of some family member who has distinguished him- or herself. We might also be ashamed about someone who is regarded as an embarrassment.

When we get married, we come with whatever family we have, and how we go on relating to them has to become part of the family history that our wedding creates.

Where are you now?

Who gets invited to the wedding may tell us quite a lot about our current family relationships. Most people find that costs dictate how many can be invited. But there are other factors too, and families can be amazingly unhelpful. Anthony and Julie faced a real dilemma. She was particularly close to one uncle and aunt, with whom she had lived for a while. They had split up, but obviously she wanted them both to come to her wedding. Her uncle refused to come unless his new wife (whom Julie did not know) was also invited. Nor would he come if his ex was there. Anthony and Julie ended up with neither of these people they really cared about being present. Family feuds got in the way of family happiness.

Being fair to two families can be a delicate issue. How you spend Christmas is the classic example. Unless you are going to eat two Christmas dinners, you have to choose between going to one family or neither. Taking it in turns works for some, but differences in where people live, and whether they can cope with your growing family, may complicate matters.

There are many things where families have a particular way of doing things, and negotiating whether you will do either or neither of them in your new marriage takes enormous tact.

Although the words 'forsaking all others' in the wedding vows are primarily about not being in love with someone else, it does also apply to the way we relate to parents or our families of origin and the way they relate to us. Norma's marriage did not last very long. She had lived at home, an only child, for over 30 years. Her new home was only a mile or two away. But her parents expected her to call every day, and to be there – with her new husband – for Sunday lunch. They could not let her go and she felt torn between her old home and her new one. Eventually, and sadly, the power of the old one proved stronger. The story goes that there was a suggestion that there should be a promise in the marriage service for parents to the effect of 'We promise to leave these two to get on with it *their* way'. Even if it is not part of the service, it is a good thing to agree to do. The promise that *is* in the service

> Will you, the families and friends of N *and* N,
> support and uphold them in their marriage
> now and in the years to come?
> We will.
>
> (The Declarations, The Marriage Service, p.106)

Things to talk about and share

- Who decides the guest list for the wedding, and how do you draw the line?

- When you talk about 'home' do you mean where you live now, or the place you came from?

- How do you handle differences about family rituals – for example when you open Christmas presents, or how birthdays are celebrated?

goes at least some of the way to reminding everyone that this is a new chapter, and that relationships with parents and others will need some renegotiation. You haven't stopped loving them, but you have to move on. Sometimes people have to begin their married life in the home of one set of parents. That takes special care if it is to work out properly. Jimmy and Sandra found that, although her parents were very welcoming, and gave them lots of freedom, they were very inhibited about two things in particular – making love and having rows. Those needed more privacy than the size of their house and the thickness of its walls would allow.

Things to talk about and share

- How involved do you feel you should be with problems in the families you come from?

- How might you care for your parents if they become frail? If you have to choose between their needs and yours, how would you decide?

- What family customs will you continue, and which will you change because of your marriage?

Where are you going?

Even though you may not see very much of them, you still are part of the wider family, and their stresses and strains are bound to have an impact on you. Everyone, unless they go to a desert island, will go on being part of the two circles from which they came.

People say that life is a great circle. Children are born and are very dependent on their parents. They grow up and achieve their own independence. But, as time goes on, parents begin to be dependent on their children. If they live to a ripe old age, that dependency can be considerable. Children may get to the point of worrying far more about their ageing parents than the parents ever did about their infant children. It raises the whole question of family responsibility. Families often fall out with each other because some are seen as opting out of their fair share of caring when a parent is ill, or becomes unable to manage. Those who run nursing homes tell sad stories of elderly people whose families never come near. Where families have always shared their lives and troubles, and have valued each other, it is a very different story.

Money

All that I have I share with you

(The Giving of Rings, The Marriage Service, p. 109)

'Money is the root of all evil' said the old song. Some people think that comes from the Bible, but what St Paul actually wrote to his young friend Timothy was that 'the love of money is a root of all kinds of evil'. Since the statistics show that money is one of the things most commonly argued about by couples, it looks as if he was right. It is almost as if money has to be thought about at two levels – first of all the practical

'It could be argued that the last parts of many couples to be married are their pockets. Learning to think in terms of 'ours' rather than 'mine' is a gradual process, and one that some people find quite hard to do.'

one of how we pay our bills, and then seeing what money represents to us. That could be power, or generosity, or all sorts of other things both good and bad.

Money is certainly a powerful factor in many couples' decisions – from the early days of how often you go out, and what is spent when you do, right through to major decisions like getting married, buying a house, and deciding to start to family. What we can afford, and how we cope when we cannot afford things, are a major part of how we live.

A preacher once said that the last part of an Englishman to be converted is his pocket. It could be argued that the last parts of many couples to be married are their pockets. Learning to think in terms of 'ours' rather than 'mine' is a gradual process, and one that some people find quite hard to do.

Where are you coming from?

Michael had a very easy life as a child. Whilst not being rich, his parents were comfortably off. They could go out when they chose, had a couple of holidays each year, and never had to worry about where the money was coming from. It was quite different for Judith, with whom Michael eventually fell in love. Her family was always scraping to pay the bills. They didn't always get a holiday, and Judith depended on handed-down clothes and things from the charity shops for much of her childhood. Both of their families were very happy, but money played a different role in each of them and, as a result, Michael and Judith came to adult life with very different attitudes and expectations. Putting it in its broadest terms, Michael was a spender and Judith was a saver. The reasons are obvious enough. He had never needed to save, because there always seemed to be money available. She didn't want to have the worries she saw her parents had, and so was anxious to have as big a cushion to protect them from financial crises as she could. They had to do a lot of negotiating to find the right way to handle money in their partnership.

Our financial education, if we can call it that, starts with our childhood experiences. Children don't understand the value of money, but they do understand when they are told they can't have the toy they want because it costs too much. Even that can be an issue, because some parents find it almost impossible to say 'No' to their children. If children are given pocket money and have to learn to make their choices about what to spend it on, they may learn to handle money better than those who are simply bought anything they want, or whose pocket money is supplemented if they make a mistake.

Things to talk about and share

- **What pocket money did you get when you were little? What was it for? What happened if you ran out?**

- **How aware were you of your family's financial situation?**

- **What are your feelings about having debts?**

- **What is your view on the difference between credit and debt?**

- **How do you use credit and store cards?**

There are very few young people today, especially those who have been to college, who do not start off adult life with quite considerable and unavoidable debts, to which they will have to add if they are to have a reliable car, to say nothing of their own housing. It may not be possible, even if we wanted to, to live in the same way as the older generation, who, with comparatively little money, were able nonetheless to say that they had never been in debt. They rejected buying things on hire purchase, and did without until there was the money in the bank. Owing anything was a frightening and bad thing in their eyes. Today, credit may be the positive means that enables things to begin. The problem is when credit becomes debt. Credit enables: debt destroys.

Where are you now?

If you are about to get married, there will be huge extra pressures on your finances, even if some of the costs of the wedding are being met by others. There are so many ways of organizing everyday finances. Some people have a joint account, others two separate accounts, yet others have both. There are no right and wrong ways of doing it – but how we arrange things may be significant. Having just one account might make things like buying each other presents difficult. Having two accounts might make budgeting complicated unless you regularly compare notes and sort things out. Derrick and Fiona said they could never have a joint account, because they didn't trust each other enough. Their judgement may be based on their real experience but, if they can't trust each other with money, can they really trust each other for life?

Some couples start out together with financial help from one of their families. This can be both enabling and difficult at the same time. A loan from a family member is treated differently from a loan from the bank. There is no interest to be paid, but repaying the capital can be a problem in the long term. It can also complicate family relationships. Gemma and Vic were so grateful to his father for a substantial loan that enabled them to put a down payment on their first flat. But it made Gemma's parents, who had much less money, feel that they had somehow let their daughter down because they had not been able to contribute.

For most people, having two incomes is more or less essential. But, if people are living up to the hilt of both incomes, what will happen if one of them isn't available? Job security is not what it used to be, and many people will have times when one or other is out of work. Sickness benefits don't replace income in the long term, and that also may create an unavoidable drain on your usual resources. There may be time on one income, or a reduced second income if you take time out from a career to look after children.

You may want to consider whether taking out household and life insurances is a worthwhile investment, even if they are a drain on the purse. They are obligatory if you have a mortgage, but for those who are renting their home, or living with family, there is a choice. What would happen if you were burgled, or there was a fire? Life insurance may be a security against the worst happening.

Things to talk about and share

- **Are you both happy about the way you organize your money?**

  - **Will you want to change anything when you get married? How?**

- **How do you make decisions about major purchases?**

- **What are your ground rules for the way you use a joint account?**

- **Which things do you think of as 'yours' and 'mine' and which are 'ours'?**

- **What is the difference between needing something and wanting something?**

- **How do you make decisions about how much (if anything) to spend on each other's birthday and Christmas presents?**

- **Do you have the right insurance for your present needs?**

For people who are in second marriages, money matters can be even more complex. There may be money to be paid in maintenance. Your new partner will have to come to terms with those regular outgoings as part of forming this new relationship. That is another example of where feelings about money can be as significant as the actual cash.

In some countries prenuptial agreements are made, with formal decisions about what will happen to property and assets if the marriage ends. Such things fly in the face of the vows that say the marriage is 'till death us do part'.

Where are you going?

Financial planning has become a big business, and preparing for retirement is increasingly important even from the early years of marriage. For many 'chance would be a fine thing' because there is no spare cash for such long-term needs. But, if there is any possibility of being able to help children through further education, or give them a start in getting into the housing market, most parents would want to do so. In previous generations, it was fine to think in terms of what you would eventually leave to children in your will, but the chances are that their greatest times of need will be long before you die. And for yourselves, retirement will come, and some sort of provision needs to be made.

Inevitably, we think most of all about outgoings, but there will also be income coming in – maybe some of it unexpectedly, in the way of money left to us. How we handle these 'bonuses' can be tricky. A contestant on a television quiz show was asked how he would spend his winnings. Although he was a husband and father, the money was all going to be spent on things for himself. Getting financial advice, even if you can't take it immediately, is worthwhile.

Budgeting is a delicate art – there are so many things to be included. One item you might not have considered is budgeting for what you give away. We are, on the whole, a generous nation, as the amazing amounts raised for 'Children in Need' and similar events prove. But that is giving provoked by a sponsored happening, or by a special event. What is even better is the steady giving month by month or year by year when people have identified a cause they really want to support. Charities can reclaim the tax you have paid on your gift when it is donated formally: they can't when it is dropped in a bucket. There are encouragements to regular giving through Payroll Giving and other schemes. When couples are committed to whatever it is they support, it becomes part of their marriage, part of their way of life.

Things to talk about and share

- Have you made any long-term financial plans for yourselves, for children and/or retirement?

- If Great-Aunt Jemima left you £500,000, what would you do?

  - What would you do if she left you £500?

  - In either case, would you think of it as 'my' money, or 'ours'?

- What causes do you support, or might you support, on a regular basis?

- How will you decide on the amount you give?

Roles

Marriage is intended by God to be a creative relationship, as his blessing enables husband and wife to love and support each other in good times and in bad, and to share in the care and upbringing of children.

(Pastoral Introduction, The Marriage Service, p. 102)

The committee is meeting to arrange the village fête. The discussion centres on who is going to do what. 'Fred will want to do the beer tent', says someone, 'he's done it since his father died, and his father did it for as long as anyone can remember.' The role Fred has to play seems to have been designated for him from birth. Others' roles are not so preordained. Julie is going to do the children's fancy dress because Rita promised she could have a turn. Bob is going to organize the raffle because he knows how to deal with the paperwork. But can they find anyone to look after the car park? No one wants to do it. George gets landed with it because he wasn't at the meeting. They all know he won't speak to them for ages, but they can take it!

A life together isn't all that different from the fête. There are jobs to be done – the only difference is that the committee had twelve members, and a marriage has only two. Ogden Nash, as always, has a verse to offer:

> *Once there was a man named Palliser,*
> > *and he asked his wife, May I be a gourmet?*
> *And she said, You sure may.*
> *But she also said, If my kitchen*

> *is going to produce a Cordon Blue*
> *It won't be me, it will be you.*
> *And he said, you mean Cordon Bleu?*
> *And she said to never mind the pronunciation*
> *so long as it was him and not heu.*
>
> (from 'The strange case of Mr Palliser's palate')

The roles we are called on to play in a marriage can be as high-flown as provider and homemaker, or as down-to-earth as who empties the bins. There is no reason to suppose that roles, once defined, have to remain the same for ever. It is all part of the ongoing negotiations that all living relationships need to have. What is certainly true is that couples expect more of each other than previous generations, because there are fewer other family members available to share out those roles.

'In today's world, virtually no task is gender-specific.'

Where are you coming from?

In today's world, virtually no task is gender-specific. The woman may be the qualified accountant, and the man the expert cook. Every job that is to be done, apart from giving birth and breastfeeding, is open to both partners.

A generation or so back, roles were clearly defined. Men were the breadwinners, went out to work, came home and were waited on. They did the household accounts, mowed the lawn and did any minor repairs that were needed. They did not cook, change nappies or iron shirts. Women kept house, looked after the children, cleaned, cooked and washed up, and made clothes. They did not do evening classes in car maintenance or elementary plumbing.

It is useful to look back to see how household duties were managed in the places you grew up. It is unlikely that you will want the same divisions of labour as your parents had –
still less your grandparents' way of doing things. Behind every resentment that 'he/she doesn't . . .' may lurk a memory of how things used to be. The divisions don't have to be equal, unless you want them to be. But they do need to be mutually agreed. If not, someone is going to feel aggrieved or put upon.

Colin and Bernice both had demanding jobs, leaving home by half past seven in the morning, and rarely getting home before half past seven in the evening. Neither of them

Things to talk about and share

- **How do you define a 'domestic chore'?**

  - **How were those tasks shared in the home where you grew up?**

  - **Did that suit everyone involved?**

  - **How would you have liked them to be different?**

enjoyed cooking, and so they relied on ready-cooked meals and takeaways. Although that suited them both, Bernice in her heart of hearts felt guilty, because her mother had been a fantastic cook, and had spent a lot of effort teaching Bernice how to follow in her footsteps. It was only when she was able to tell Colin how she felt that they were able to find a way round her negative feelings. He took on more than the half share he had previously had of chores at the weekend, so that, at least once a week, she could use the skills in the kitchen of which she was actually quite proud. Roles, and expectations about them, can come from within ourselves, as well as from our partners and parents.

Think also about the other roles in your home. Who was the peace-maker? Who was the maker and enforcer of rules?

Where are you now?

If you are living together, you will already have worked out who does what. Ideally, those decisions suit you both, at least for the time being. Think about those more profound roles that one of the marriage service prayers mentions – being 'a strength in need, a counsellor in perplexity, a comfort in sorrow and a companion in joy'. Professional counsellors some-times talk about the 'marital fit'. There are ways in which you complement each other, and so fit together to make a satisfying unit. Maybe it is a bit like being

Things to talk about and share

- **What do you think your strengths and weaknesses are?**

- **How do you think your strengths and weaknesses complement each other?**

- **Do you both feel the balance of household tasks is OK for you?**

- **Who does the jobs that neither of you likes doing?**

pieces of a jigsaw puzzle. By interlocking we make a good picture. If you have been together for a while, you may have seen those roles shifting from one to the other. Perhaps at first you were the dependent one, looking for strength, but have now found it – and in turn can offer it to your partner when they feel in need. Some joys and sorrows come to you both equally but, at other times, it is a personal thing, and you need to lean on your other half. Knowing you have someone who can provide what you need at that moment is a tremendous strength.

Where are you going?

Some people worry that, when they marry, their roles that suit them well now will change. But changing circumstances often involve changing roles. The arrival of a family is the biggest one, and can be a particular challenge to men. With the best will in the world, their wife isn't going to be able to pay them the attention that she might have done in the past. Babies are exhausting, and especially if their care is being combined with employment, the amount of time for just the two of you is going to be very limited. For Andy and Lesley, it was the cause of their splitting up. In his head, Andy knew that Lesley was just too busy to give him all the attention he craved. But he couldn't translate that into patience to wait for easier times. The baby felt like a rival, and what is more, a rival who was winning the competition for Lesley's affection. He loved them both, but he could not cope with sharing Lesley, even with the child he loved.

New roles may be forced on couples by having to care for ageing parents, or other family members who become ill. New work commitments may mean that the patterns that have worked so well are no longer appropriate. One or other of you may be called on to work some evenings, or weekends, or to travel abroad on business for significant amounts of time. It can work the other way round as well. Suzie and Will had a kind of semi-detached marriage at first, because he spent every third week in the US, and was away from home at least two nights a week for the rest of the time. When he got a promotion that meant he was based totally at the head office in the UK, Suzie found it quite hard to have him at home so much. She had developed a lifestyle that often did not have to take account of him – and now he wanted her to be around to do things together.

Things to talk about and share

- How flexible are you – do you prefer things to be predictable or spontaneous?

- How will you handle changing circumstances, like children and new work commitments?

- As you look forward, what are the possible new roles you find exciting or challenging?

Some couples make major changes in the way they divide responsibilities. When Eric and Brenda had their first child, they decided that, since they both enjoyed their jobs, but did not want their child to be cared for by others, they would see if it was possible to job-share. That worked well and, although they had a reduced income, they both felt fulfilled at work and at home, with one of them working three days, and the other two. Other couples find role reversals forced on them by redundancies. Di had stopped work as a nurse to look after the children but, when Glenn lost his job, she found it easier to get employment than he did, and so he became a very happy house husband.

Sex

**The gift of marriage brings
husband and wife together
in the delight and tenderness of sexual union
and joyful commitment to the end of their lives.**

(Preface to The Marriage Service, p. 105)

Sexual attraction is at the very heart of marriage. If that were not the case, people would stay 'just friends'. When sex is good, it is part of the most sublime feelings of closeness and intimacy that human beings can experience. It is a language of touch and excitement, of gentleness and passion, that says things that words cannot begin to say. When it is not good, it can bring sadness and disappointment. Like many wonderful things, it can be abused and become something destructive instead of creative.

Our sexuality is at the centre of our understanding of ourselves. The question on most forms after asking our name is whether we are male or female. We start the process of discovering what that means from the moment we are born and, although the experts differ on how much is 'nature' and how much is 'nurture', we come to adult life having a reasonable idea of what being a man or a woman means for us personally. For the majority, that will lead us into making sexual relationships with people of the opposite sex, although there are minorities whose natural inclination is to form same-sex partnerships, who can feel drawn to people of either sex, and also some who make a decision, consciously or otherwise, not to form any partnerships at all.

The Christian community, sadly, has not always had very positive attitudes to God's gift of sexuality. The old marriage service talks about marriage being not '. . . to satisfy men's carnal lusts and appetites, like brute beasts that have no understanding'.[1] But, as the quotation from the modern service above shows, we have moved on from those times, and we need to be saying clearly that the gift of sex is something, holy, God-given and good. No amount of misuse of it can take away from that truth.

Where are you coming from?

The attitudes to sex in the homes where we grew up will have had their effect on us. Those who brought us up will have been deeply affected by the people who brought *them* up and so, in this area, we are often working with feelings that come from a long way back. All sorts of things may be indicators. In some families nudity is treated as natural in the home, in others there is almost an obsession about avoiding it. How you feel about your body in adult life – whether it is the right shape or size in your opinion – can add to those childhood ideas.

Amazingly, there are still many girls who are not prepared by their parents for the beginning of their periods, and an even larger number of boys receive no sex education at home. Sex education in schools is much better than it was, but there are no guarantees that it answers the real questions that young people have. It tends to be better on the mechanical than on the emotional and relational aspects of sex. Mike and Julie had three children by the time they were 18 and, when asked whether they intended the fourth that was on the way, she said: 'I don't know why it keeps happening.' Kevin and Mandy had been married 18 months, and were worried that they had not conceived a child. It turned out that they had never had full intercourse. When they tried, she yelped. He didn't want to hurt her, and so they continued to have lots of sexual fun and closeness, but not intercourse. Both couples came from families where sex was never mentioned. But in both cases, they were hardly 'shrinking violets'. One man had been a boy soldier, and the other was a Territorial Army NCO. If people slip through the sex education net, with neither home nor school being a place to get good information, then the result is usually *mis*-information. I used to run sessions on contraception in a military college for sixteen- to seventeen-year-olds. Over many years, I would break the ice by getting them to tell me what physical changes had happened to them at puberty. Almost without exception, I was given wrong information, which the others did not challenge. Ignorance is not bliss, but is surprisingly common.

We also bring our personal history of experimentation. There is an old saying that '95 per cent of men admit they masturbate, and the other 5 per cent are liars'. That is probably not far from the mark and, although that was said about men, it is unlikely to be very different for women. That is part of our self-discovery but, as so often with sexual matters, it is the feelings that lie behind it that are more significant – guilt and secrecy, for example. Our first experiences with someone else form part of our history. Sex is built up in many teenagers' minds as something that is fantastic but, in practice, the first fumbling attempts are often disappointing – but you can't admit that to anyone!

Sex involves a great deal of trust – we often use the imagery of being naked to imply vulnerability. In an age where many couples come together having had previous sexual partners, that has particular importance. A government advertising campaign at the outbreak of the HIV/AIDS pandemic read 'Every time you sleep with a boy, you sleep with all his old girlfriends'. Sexual honesty can sometimes be very demanding. Wendy got a terrible shock when, soon after her marriage, she found she had contracted a sexually transmitted disease. At first she thought that Barry had had an affair, and it was with some difficulty that she came to terms with the fact that he had

Things to talk about and share

- **Where did you get your sex education?**
  - **What part did your home play in that?**
  - **In what ways would you want it to be different for any children you might have?**
- **How relaxed or otherwise are you about being naked? Do you like your body?**
- **Have previous experiences coloured the way you think about sex?**
- **Are there any difficult things from the past you want to share with each other?**

contracted the infection long before they had met, but had never dared to tell her.

Those who make new partnerships after a previous marriage or long-term relationship also bring their memories, both good and bad, of what sex was like in those partnerships. Accepting that things are bound to be different in bed with a new partner is just one of the many adjustments they make as they create a new life together.

For a very small group of people, where they are coming from is a very painful place, because there has been sexual abuse of some kind. The evidence is that, somewhere down the line, this is going to come out, and for couples to hold secrets like that from each other, whilst very understandable, is probably not going to be good for either of them. Paula's abuse by her step-father only became known to her husband Guy when their daughter reached the age that Paula had been when the abuse started, and she became obsessively overprotective. Guy suddenly felt that she had been holding him at arm's length for all the years they had been together, whereas before he had thought they had had no secrets. They needed to find help to cope with it all. Had they been able to share things earlier, it would have saved them both a lot of pain.

Where are you now?

It usually takes a while for a couple to settle into a sex life that is satisfying for them both. Initially, there may be lots of excitement of discovery and getting to know each other, and that should lead into a real understanding of what gives pleasure. But people sometimes are so concerned not to be critical, that they fail to tell the truth. Will and Ruth were a case in point. They had been together for a couple of years and Will thought their sex life was great. But in talking before their marriage, Ruth suddenly burst out, saying she felt that he was using her for his pleasure, and was totally unaware of her needs. Needless to say, Will was totally thrown by this, and they had some hard talking to do to think things through more honestly. The end result was a better sexual relationship for them both. They were able to get through that on their own but, for many, it would be a situation where professional help would make a difference.

Things to talk about and share

- **What are the best things about your sex life now?**

- **Are there things you would like to suggest to each other that are different?**

- **What are your 'yuk barriers'?**

- **What does sex add to your whole relationship?**

- **What words do you use for your 'bits'?**

It has often been said, correctly, that the most important sex organ is the brain. There is no end to what the imagination can provide to fulfil our sexual needs. It is a physical language to use to communicate with each other, just as words are a language. And all languages have to be learned, and constantly change. So, in sexual terms, there are so many things that have the potential to give pleasure – but none of them are automatic. Everyone has what one sex therapist called their 'yuk barrier' – things that may be exciting and good for someone else, but turn *them* off completely.

Whether sex for you is daily, and spontaneous and full of variety, or regular on Saturdays and utterly predictable, is of little importance, as long as it is what suits you both. As in everything else, there has to be room for compromise. As long as you are able to ask each other for what you want, and can cope if that is not something the other feels comfortable with, then things will be good. But some couples who in other ways are very open with each other find asking for things sexually quite daunting. The more you can be open, the closer you can be. Maybe you always make love in bed – but one of you would like to be on the living room carpet, or outdoors somewhere private. Maybe you never have a bath together, or massage each other, but one of you would love to, but doesn't like to suggest it. The possibilities are endless, but only if you are able to ask. Bob and Charmian were a couple who found that hard – strangely – because he was a doctor and she was a physiotherapist. They were both used to bodies and knew all the facts. Maybe it was because they usually dealt with other people's bodies in a clinical way that they found it very hard to be uninhibited and relaxed with each other. By facing up to their problem, they soon found it was possible to change, and things improved rapidly.

Where are you going?

Most young people find it hard to imagine older people's sex lives – it is something for the young, athletic and beautiful. But, of course, that is not the case and, for most people, sex will continue to be a part of their life together right to the end. But age brings changes in every part of life. Henry remarried later in life and was very distressed that he literally could not keep up with his new wife's sexual demands. It took a little gentle reasoning for both of them to see that at 83 (and his wife was 81) they couldn't expect his body to behave the way it did when he was 23.

Age and illness can have various effects. Sex after the menopause may be different: some women find they lubricate less easily. Most men will experience some degree of impotence as time goes on, either temporarily on the grand scale, or, more generally, in losing the degree of hardness of erection they were used to. However, fear of impotence causes more problems than the real thing. A one-off problem, stemming from tiredness or alcohol, can turn into a real fear that it will always happen. Some diseases, or drugs taken over a long period, may have effects on sexual functioning as well. None of these things are a barrier to ongoing sexual happiness but may need some discussion with the doctor and a lot of sympathetic understanding from each other.

Things to talk about and share

- **How do you feel about the idea of older people making love?**

- **Would you be able to share with each other any sexual problems that age or illness might bring?**

Tom Lehrer wrote a song that was a plea to his lover for good sex now, which included the words below. That was fine – but he was wrong about old age. We are sexual beings from the day we are born to the day we die.

So let's act with agility
While we still have facility
For we'll soon reach senility
And lose the ability.[2]

Starting again

*Make their life together a sign of Christ's love
in this broken and disordered world,
that unity may overcome estrangement,
forgiveness heal injury
and joy overcome despair.*

(Additional Prayers, The Marriage Service, p. 159)

There are very few people who come to marriage today who have not had previous relationships. One or both may have been married before. Those marriages may have been ended by death, or divorce. Many will have had a long-term relationship – perhaps several. In one way or another, and at different levels, those relationships that have ended may represent sadness, tragedy, hurt, betrayal and failure. Most people know something about the 'broken and disordered world', the 'estrangement, injury and despair' of that prayer from the marriage service.

But the new relationship they now have represents the other side of that equation – the 'unity, forgiveness and joy' that can transform the bad things. Christians believe that is what God's love can do for any of us.

Where are you coming from?

Although the past may have some hurts, most people bring joys as well as sorrows to their new relationship. Even marriages that have ended bitterly will have had times of great joy and hope. One of the most positive things in developing new relationships will be incorporating those good memories from the past into the new hopes for the future.

Martina had a rough deal. As a teenager, she got involved with a boy who was on drugs. They married, much against her parents' wishes and within a year she had to escape from a situation that became impossible for her. She lived for a while in a refuge but, eventually, long after her divorce, she met another man who seemed to her the very opposite of what she had known in her first marriage. For a while things seemed to be all she had hoped for, but then she became the victim of the most modern threat to marriage – the Internet affair. Her husband not only left her, but emigrated to live with someone he had never actually met. By the time she met Alan, her self-worth was very low indeed. To be rejected in favour of photographs and text messages really knocks the way you think about yourself. It took a very special kind of man, like Alan, to enable her to move on. The past seemed to overshadow her, and he had to learn how to live with her ghosts, and gradually to exorcize them.

Things to talk about and share

- **What are the good things you bring from past relationships?**

- **What did you enjoy most about being on your own?**

- **Do you know your own 'sensitive areas' caused by events in your past?**

  - **Do you know your partner's?**

- **Are there any skeletons in the cupboard that you have not shared?**

  - **Why are they so hard to talk about?**

Being able to share the hurts – perhaps not as complex or terrible as Martina's – is basic to building a new relationship of trust. Some secrets are very hard to share. Victims of sexual abuse or rape usually find it hard to share what has happened to them, even with someone they trust and love. But events that scar us deeply can affect us in unexpected ways, as Denise found when her husband bought a new sweater. She became very upset – and it was only after a lot of thought that she realized that this new item was the same colour as her rapist had been wearing. Max found it hard to tell his fiancée that he had a brother who had been convicted of a paedophile offence. It had made him ill at ease with children, as if his brother's crime was somehow contagious.

Churches vary in how they approach those marrying again. Gaynor was grateful that the forms that the Church of England usually asks couples to complete in this situation enabled her to take the process of letting go of the past a stage further. At first she had thought it was 'raking up the past', but realized that it was another way in which she and her new partner could be totally honest with each other. Some of the issues those forms raise, such as what provision there is for any children of former marriages, apply equally to provision for children born outside marriage. If you want to see those forms, you can download them from the Church of England web site (see 'Resources' for further details).

What we bring from the past doesn't have to be negative. Arthur had had a wonderful marriage of over 40 years. His wife died from cancer and a few years later he met Betty, a widow who also had had a very happy marriage. They had high expectations for their new relationship. But both of them had to work at the fact that it was new and not just a replacement for the old. They had to learn to be able to talk about their deceased partners without the other feeling that comparisons were being made. As they said of their new marriage: 'It isn't better or worse – it is different.'

Where are you now?

The law talks about people being 'free to marry'. That is about being old enough, not being married already, and so on. Beyond that are the internal laws that each of us has, about whether we feel 'free to marry'. Craig was divorced, and legally free to marry. But the cause of the divorce had been his violence, and the things that made him like that had not been ended by a court decree. He was now planning his marriage to Faith, with whom he was living – indeed with whom he already had a child. But from time to time his self-control went, and he beat her up. This came out in the talks they had with their vicar, and they began to try to find ways of getting help. They came to the conclusion that it would be better to put off the wedding for a while until they saw whether things were changing. He worked hard with a professional therapist and, a year later than the original date planned, a wonderful wedding day was had by all. He was by then much more 'free to marry' than he had been before.

One or both of you may already have children from previous relationships. Helping two sets of children to become a new family can be tricky, as can becoming a step-parent, or a parent's new partner. These days it is often called 'blending families' – and, as in cooking, blending takes some skill. Parents normally learn their trade as they go along, but one of you may be catapulted into being a parent figure for a teenager without any previous experience. Sometimes all the children will be living in, or be based at, the new home of their parents. Others will be regular or irregular visitors. Helping them all to feel they belong is a great art. Step-parents find that making and enforcing the household rules is one of the most difficult things to get right. Children are all too happy to say 'You're not my real Dad or Mum – you can't tell me what to do.'

Being a step-parent can feel as if it has all the stresses and strains of parenting magnified several times over. In all the busyness and complexity of new families, time for yourselves just as a couple may be difficult to find. But, because of the extra demands on you both, it is vital to find such times for togetherness.

Things to talk about and share

- **If one or both of you has children already, how are you involving them in this new marriage?**

- **How will they be involved in the service?**

- **Do the children have contact with their absent parent, and his or her family?**

- **How will you handle discipline with step-children?**

- **Are there things that make you less 'free to marry' than you would wish?**

Where are you going?

The more complicated your past, the more complicated your future! If you think ahead from your own marriage to those of your children – with whom will your daughter walk down the aisle? Her natural father, her step-father, or neither of them? It is not just weddings, but other great family events that may raise questions about how the past is allowed to be part of your future without ill feelings or rivalries.

Particularly when people enter into second marriage later in life, there needs to be thought about how the various children figure in your will. Children who have grown up with an expectation that one day they will have an injection of finance from your estate may feel unhappy about it all going to a surviving partner whom, maybe, they hardly know, and who has his or her own family to leave it to. It is perhaps an area where prenuptial contracts can play a useful part. Carl and Davina were delighted that his father was getting married again, but were very worried that his new wife, who did not get on with them, might acquire not only his money when he died, but also their family heirlooms – not things of great monetary value, but which were part of the family history.

Things to talk about and share

- Will your existing families affect your decision to have more children?

- Who will go to, or be invited to, future family events?

- What provision have you made for all the family in your will?

Ingredients of the wedding cake

In thinking about your wedding service, the principles of 'Where are you coming from?', 'Where are you now?' and 'Where are you going?' that have shaped the rest of this book still apply. Each of you will have memories of weddings you have attended. They may have provided you with ideas of what you want to happen at your own. Your parents will have ideas that come from memories of their weddings and, whilst you will want to listen to those, you need to hang on to the fact that this is *your* wedding, and not an action replay of theirs. You will probably have some definite ideas about how this great event is linked to your present life, and dreams about how it will launch you into a new stage of your relationship in the future.

This chapter is assuming that you want to get married in church, although there may be ideas here that would apply even in a civil ceremony. Every denomination, and indeed each individual church, will have its own ways of doing things. Some things may not be physically possible in some buildings. But, if you think of your wedding day as a wonderful cake, here are some of the ingredients you might want to think about putting into it.

Because this book comes from a Church of England publisher, and is written by a Church of England vicar, some of the possibilities are specific to Anglican services. But most of it will apply whatever the denomination of the church in which you get married. You will need to discuss with the people where you marry what is possible, and how things you would like might be incorporated.

Although we have to use legally approved forms of service, this is *your* wedding – a unique occasion. Taking time to plan it will make it even more special for you both. At the end of the day, the minister will have to agree to every detail.

Music

The thing that sets the tone for the service is the music that is played as the bride, or the bride and groom, enters. There will be other opportunities for music later, whilst registers are signed,

Things to talk about and decide

- **What music do we want**
  - **as people are arriving?**
  - **when the bride, or bride and groom, enters?**
  - **during the signing of the register?**
  - **as people leave?**
- **Do we have friends who could take part in this way?**

and everyone will leave with some more music ringing in their ears. Your chosen music will add a lot to the sense of occasion, and may be one of the ways in which you make it very personal. Some churches have the means to play recorded music, but for most, you will be enjoying live music. Talk to the organist, and take his or her advice. Some splendid pieces of music do not work on very small organs – they would sound silly. Be aware too that not all organists can play anything set in front of them. Better to have something less showy played well than a virtuoso piece played badly. There are many discs of 'Wedding Music' available to give you ideas. You may want to incorporate other live music – maybe you would like friends who play or sing to take part. See what is possible in your particular church.

Order of service

Most denominations have a service book, which will provide you with the basic shape of the service. The Church of England's *Common Worship* marriage service has within it a large number of possible variations and, in addition,

Things to talk about and decide

- **Which order of service do we want to use?**

- **Would we want to receive Holy Communion as part of the service?**

you are still entitled to use the service from the 1662 *Book of Common Prayer*, or the version of it produced in 1928, and which, in its present form, is known as Series One. Talk to the people at your church and read through the various possibilities. There is material available on the FLAME web site (see 'Resources' at the end of this book), which may help guide you through the wonderful range of choices offered by *Common Worship*. There are choices of Preface, forms of the Vows, words at the Giving of the Ring(s), and the Blessing of the Marriage, amongst others. The service you end up with may well be a unique mix of those choices: hymns, readings and music – different from any wedding there has ever been before.

If you are both used to receiving Holy Communion, that is a great way for couples to be aware of Christ's presence as they begin this new stage of their life together. It need not lengthen the service unduly. Sometimes just the bride and groom receive Communion, but, more usually, anyone in the congregation who wishes comes to join them at the altar.

Hymns

You don't have to sing hymns at all, of course, but most people want to. The number of hymns will depend on how the whole service is devised. Most people have three or four. The vital thing is that you choose hymns that people will know – there is nothing more embarrassing for the vicar than having to sing a solo. Many couples enjoy thumbing through the hymnbook seeing which hymns both of them know and like – that often cuts the choice down quite a lot! There are some excellent modern hymns written specially for weddings, and sung to very familiar tunes, which are worth considering. Once you have chosen what you want, discuss with the clergy where each of them fits best within the service.

Things to talk about and decide

- **What is our shortlist of possible hymns that we both like?**

- **Are any of them 'must-haves'? Why?**

Readings

You need to choose at least one reading from the Bible. *Common Worship* provides 22 suggestions – but you can use another passage from the Bible if it means something special to you. People also like to have other readings that are personal favourites – poems or extracts from other books. Discuss them with whoever is conducting your service. They will need to agree to them, and may well want to incorporate things from them in whatever they say in the sermon. The Internet has several good sites with anthologies of wedding poems for you to browse through.

Things to talk about and decide

- **Which reading(s) from the Bible do we want?**

- **Are there poems or other readings we want to include?**

- **Who is going to read them?**

Prayers

One or two of the prayers in the service will be 'compulsory', but most remain your choice. *Common Worship* provides 14 pages of possible prayers for you to choose from – and you are not even limited to those, if there are other prayers that you wish to include. If you want to pray for particular things or people, talk about it to whoever is taking the service. You may, for example, want to mention a

Things to talk about and decide

- **Which prayers do we want to use?**

- **Are there special things or people we would like to be mentioned?**

- **Do we want to write a prayer ourselves to include in the service?**

family member who is ill, or who lives abroad, and so cannot be present. You can write your own prayers, or it may be the tradition in your church for a time when anyone in the congregation can lead everyone in prayer in their own words.

Registers

The laws about registration of marriages are about to change and, although under the new rules, the registers signed in church will no longer have any legal status, it is likely that churches will go on having some informal registers to sign during or after the service. Where it happens often depends on the design of the building, and there may be a choice open to you. Where it happens may also define *when* it happens. Talk to your minister about how it works in your church.

Things to talk about and decide

■ **Who do we want to sign the register as witnesses?**

Choreography

That may sound a funny word to use – but there are many occasions during the service when people move around that benefit from thinking through in advance. As you will have noticed already, the bride can come in escorted by her father, mother, or some other family member. Alternatively, the bride and groom can enter together. Some find that more appropriate when they have been living together for some years. You will also need to decide who else is going to be in that procession – bridesmaids, page boys, maids of honour and so on – and where they are going to sit.

Depending on your church building, and the way the service is arranged, it may be possible for the couple to sit down for parts of the service.

No one has to be 'given away' these days. But the traditional ceremony is available for those who want it, and most do. An alternative is now provided where all the parents say they entrust their son and daughter to each other. Some couples find that a useful way of getting round the problem of how to involve both parents and step-parents.

The best man – who these days is sometimes a best woman – is usually the person who hands over the ring(s), but it can be

Things to talk about and decide

- **Who will be in the procession at the beginning of the service?**

- **Where will any attendants sit?**

- **Do you want to sit down for the readings and sermon?**

- **Is there to be a 'giving away', or the parental 'entrusting'?**

- **Will you have one ring or two – and who will hand them over?**

anyone. He is also a useful person to organize the movement of family if they need to gather where the registers are being signed. Ushers have an important part to play in making sure people are welcomed and know where to sit.

These are just a few starter questions to the many decisions that add up to your special day. Take your time over making them, and discuss them with all the people involved at the church. They want everything to be right for you as well. Have a wonderful day – and a wonderful life together!